HOW TO SURVIVE

WORKING FOR GOD

BY TYLER RICHARDSON

Published by Not Much of a Reader Co.
A Harp & Bowl Company
Cleveland, Tennessee — United States

First Edition: August 2025
ISBN: 979-8-218-73797-9

Disclaimer: The insights and suggestions in this book are based on personal experience, biblical study, and observations from ministry life. Every ministry context is unique. What works in one situation may not work in another. Please use discernment and seek wise counsel when applying these principles to your specific circumstances. The author and publisher make no guarantees and assume no responsibility for any outcomes resulting from the use of this material.

This book is intended for informational and inspirational purposes only. The author and publisher do not warrant the completeness or accuracy of the content.

ENDORSEMENTS

"This book would've made me go keto in the garden."
— Eve, First Woman & Inventor of Regret

"There's no book with a chapter on step-parenting the Messiah... but if there had been, it would've been in here."
— Joseph, Carpenter & Earthly Father of Jesus

"It doesn't cover everything about slaying giants or avoiding rooftop bathtubs—but the mindset tips are on point."
— David, Shepherd, King, Amateur Musician

"A fantastic survival guide for anyone feeling stuck in a whale— or just trying to make sense of divine detours."
— Jonah, Reluctant Prophet & Marine Mammal Enthusiast

"Wish I'd read the chapter on emotional regulation before the ear incident."
— Peter, Disciple, Former Fisherman & Unlicensed Ear Surgeon

"If I'd had this book before I built the ark, I might have avoided a few sleepless nights—and possibly some soggy paperwork."
— Noah, Ark Builder & Amateur Meteorologist

"This book offers wise counsel for anyone managing a tent ministry—if only it existed before my 40 years in the wilderness."
— Moses, Master of Patience

For the ones who've fallen six times—
and still stood up a seventh.

FOREWORD

Dear reader,

There are a few things you should know about the person who wrote this book. You may already know he has the voice of an angel. He is the strange kind of genius who is actually good at almost everything. He has decades of experience in basically every tiny corner and crevice of ministry. And perhaps most notably, he has amazing hair. If you know that much, you are probably also aware of how much he has cringed at my opening paragraph.

But there are a few things you don't know. And I think you should know them before you begin.

He knows all the N'SYNC choreography and most of Michael Jackson's. He once wore a show choir sequin vest and a bandana *(a la Justin Timberlake)* to a dance in middle school. In college, he marched himself to the front desk at the Disney headquarters, announcing to the receptionist he would one day be the head of the Walt Disney Company and needed to know who to speak to about starting. He spent a lot of time with his grandparents, and he knows every line to every episode of Golden Girls. He is, to say the least, not predictable. And you're guaranteed to be entertained reading this book.

On a more serious note, he has a daughter who frequently wakes up in the middle of the night and only a drive will soothe her back to sleep. Night after night, he scoops her up with a smile, tells her she looks beautiful and drives her until she falls back to sleep. On the subject of driving, he's taken countless cross-country road trips with his wife and never once has she been anywhere but the passenger seat. He does most of the laundry and most of the dishes, too. He says dinner is delicious every night *(even when it isn't)*.

The night his wife went into labor, he didn't leave her side for a moment, not even for a bathroom break.

He's been ahead of his time his entire life, AKA: he has been misunderstood since... forever. He is at home amongst the wallflowers and he spots them in every room.

He has been acknowledged with great accolade in fancy green rooms with catered meals and thanked quietly in teeny tiny church fellowship halls with sub sandwiches *(he prefers the latter by a longshot)*. He's had the joy of being honored by personal heroes and the crushing blow of disappointing those he most wanted to impress. He's felt both the highs of ministry and is all too acquainted with the incredibly low lows of the wounds so often accompanied by it.

After all that, he's remained a humble, kind man who loves Jesus deeply and truly.

He's always been a visionary. He's become a man of great integrity.

The words you're about to read come from a deep, pure and trusted well. You can take my word for it, I'm married to him.

- Kennedy Richardson

TABLE OF CONTENTS

NAMELESS + FACELESS

———

the people you can't identify

Throughout this book, I'll be recounting various stories I've heard and experienced in **over 20 years of ministry.**

It's important to me that you understand the message... without getting caught up on the messenger.

To honor the original people and places, almost every name I use will be fabricated.

I get the curiosity.

I know how tempting it can be to try and crack the code —
- *Who is he really talking about?"*
- *"What church is he referencing?"*

But I want to assure you: If I refer to someone as Pastor Tim, that doesn't mean their real name is Pastor Tom :)

LEADERSHIP LENSES

---

how to approach this book

There are some studies that suggest **up to 1,500 pastors leave the ministry every month.**

Yes... you read that correctly.
Every single month.

And that's not counting those without the title *"pastor"* — people serving in ministry every week on and off the platform. So the real number leaving ministry each month could actually be far higher.

What causes this?

What makes someone who once felt called by God to serve others... to suddenly throw in the towel?

We've all heard the stories—people of faith publicly deconstructing, ministers we admire falling from the pedestals they were placed on.

These stories might not be the norm, but they happen often enough to make anyone pause before jumping too deep into the *"ministry machine"*.

Over the next several pages, my aim is simple: To offer a life raft for those who feel like they're sinking <u>*and*</u> a strong iron sailing vessel for those just beginning their voyage into ministry waters.

This is a framework of practical methods.

Ways to approach ministry with a sober outlook, instead of a pessimistic judgment.

I call these methods: **practical gospels.**

Practical: "Capable of being done or put into effect."
Gospel: "Good news."

That's what I want this to be for you.

Good news that it's not just possible to serve God in ministry... it's possible to do it for decades.

To serve Him successfully... without falling apart, without devastation, without destroying your family or your soul.

And to do it all with genuine joy.

Too often, when people try to show empathy for the *"hard times"* in ministry, it ends up feeling laced with accusation or gossip.

That's not the point of this book.

If you're hoping for a spicy tell-all, filled with horror stories and scandal... my hope is that you'll be delightfully disappointed.

THIS IS A HOPE BOOK.

I don't shy away from reality.
I'm not afraid of it.

But I don't believe that *"reality"* automatically equals *"destiny."*

Where we are and where we've been doesn't have to determine where we're going.

There are practical things we can do — starting now —
to keep our hearts healthy and happy in ministry.

As you read, I invite you to put on imaginary glasses that I call, *"leadership lenses"*.

Look for the principles, yes, but more than that...

Ask yourself how they've already shown up in your life.
Or how they could shape your future.

You'll meet people in these pages who were hurt, but didn't quit.
People who were overwhelmed, but found their confidence again.

Remember this: **You only need one example to prove it's possible.**

Yes, there are plenty of stories of people who didn't make it.

And sadly, those stories gave others a kind of permission slip to follow the same path.

That's how graveyards of hollow greatness are made.

But examples go both ways.
We can be the other kind.

The ones who create new storylines of health, longevity, and legacy.

The kind that future generations look to and say:
"If they did it… maybe I can, too."

Let's begin!

CHAPTER ONE

ELEPHANT IN THE ROOM

---

why i say, "survive"

I wanted to start this book by addressing the potentially offensive elephant in the room: **why do I use terms like "survive" and "working for God"?**

When I say *"working for God,"* I'm referring to people who have chosen to earn their primary income through a position in a church or ministry.

This could include everyone from a church planter to a part-time social media manager, and everywhere in between.

Now, having said that, there are obviously dozens of ways you can serve a local body of believers—or be the hands and feet of Jesus around the world—without getting paid for it.

Many take on that responsibility and carry it with remarkable grace.

There are even those who fall into the bi-vocational category, working a primary job that gives them the space to serve in ministry without needing ministry funds to cover all their bills.

I don't believe one is better than the other, but I do believe they should be approached differently.

A church volunteer, for example, is balancing outside responsibilities while willingly stepping in to help serve God's house. They're not expected to *"do a job";* they're asked to help **fill a need.**

A church staff member, on the other hand, is given specific funds in exchange for a unique task they are expected to execute at a high level.

Both roles deserve patience and understanding, but they also come with different expectations.

So, if you'll indulge my language, I want to define *"working for God"* as receiving the majority of your financial livelihood from a ministry or church. Not in a way that elevates you above others, but in a way that invites conversations in your inner world you might not even realize are happening.

This book is going to address those.

Now to the second part: using the word *"survive."*

I've sat through countless meetings and services where well-established ministers and church staff took the stage and declared that serving in ministry is the highest privilege anyone could ever hope to experience.

And they're right, serving God is a privilege. So the idea that I would use a word like *"survive"* to describe ministry might make some question my love for God's people... maybe even my love for God Himself.

Honestly, I get it. **It's intense language—and that's intentional.**

Philippians 2:3–4 says: *"Do nothing out of selfish ambition or vain conceit. Rather, in humility value others above yourselves, not looking to your own interests but each of you to the interests of the others."*

This verse feels like an anthem for people who serve in ministry. They lay aside their own preferences for the sake of the Kingdom of God.

What could be more selfless than that?

So why should someone so selfless need to worry about something as seemingly selfish as trying to survive the very thing they call an honor? After all, we're part of a community that holds martyrs in the highest regard (**as we should**).

But what happens when those mindsets start to compete with each other?

Let me be clear: I love God. And I love His people.
I've been surrounded by both my whole life.

I grew up a pastor's kid. I went on youth trips, sang at conferences, spoke on panels. **I even married a worship leader for bonus points!**

I've served with various denominations and can say with confidence that I'm as comfortable in a starchy robe singing hymns as I am barefoot at a beach sunrise service. I've seen a wide range of churches—different ages, different styles, different doctrines.

And in all of it, I've seen something truly beautiful: the body of Christ, in all its intricacies.

But with those intricacies come cultures.

From culture comes values.
From values come rhythms.
From rhythms come mindsets.

And those mindsets start the domino effect.

Yet most of us are pointing at the fallen dominoes further down the line, asking, *"Why?"*

- Why does it seem like this church staff chooses ministry over their families?
- Why do I feel like my voice isn't heard in our weekly staff meeting?
- Why does it come off like my church cares more about productivity than people? Or even me, for that matter?

These questions don't just show up one day.
They are led up to by consistent, repeated surprises.

And the reason they surprise us is because we never thought we'd have to ask them. **We certainly didn't think we'd be asking them in church.** But by the time we're asking these questions, we're already far down the road.

And that's why I want to shift where we start pointing—not to pass judgment, but to get a clearer view of the root system the tree is growing from.

Because if the roots are being fed pure water, the whole tree will be healthier. **And the opposite is also true.**

The same goes for working for God.

Paul said: *"I planted the seed, Apollos watered it, but God has been making it grow." (1 Corinthians 3:6–7)*

That's what this entire book is about: **pouring clean, clear water into your soul's root system.**

It's a practical look at ministry—especially the parts you don't always equate with *"ministry."* It's a way to see the people you serve with as humans doing what they think is best. And it's a guide to help you navigate when their *"best"* doesn't exactly line up with yours.

TO THOSE WHO FEEL LIKE THEY HAVEN'T SURVIVED

Before I move on, I also want to address the silent third elephant: **the reader who already feels like they haven't survived.**

You might be thinking, *"How could I possibly start surviving now?"*

I get that.

Whether you feel like you've seen too much, or you're ashamed because you dropped the ball too many times. I know all the words

to both of those songs, and I can sing them in ten different keys.

Being around God and *"His employees"* my whole life, I've seen so many things that have inspired me deeply. I've also seen things that made me want to shut it all down and start from scratch.

And I've made mistakes. **Serious ones.**

I've had influence. I've held positions. And I've made damaging decisions that hurt my family and shaped false views of how others saw God because of me.

Those aren't things you can erase or escape with a quick fix.

I remember one season in particular. I had made some personal choices that sent my life on an up-and-down rollercoaster of freedom and shame that lasted, honestly, for years.

It all came to crashing in on me one day in the most devastating way.

But by the grace of God, and through hard conversations with my wife and painful healing, I was starting to come out the other side.

But then the ministry we worked for found out.

They discovered some of the details of my *"past struggles"*, and let's just say it didn't go well.

I'd been in tense meetings before, but this one was legendary.

When it ended, my wife and I sat in silence in the car. She gently asked if I wanted to get out of town—to go somewhere and clear my head before I spiraled into my usual pit of depression and hopelessness.

We found out there was a public tribute happening a few hours away for Billy Graham, who had just passed away. People were being allowed onto the grounds in North Carolina to pay their respects before his official funeral.

Now on the surface, this may seem unrelated, except Billy Graham had just been mentioned in that meeting we'd left.

Nearly every news outlet at the time was discussing his life and legacy. And one thing kept coming up: the fact that in all his decades of ministry, Billy Graham never had a scandal. **Not one.**

He was the most well-known minister on the planet. Even people who didn't believe in God knew who he was. He played golf with presidents, for crying out loud!

And in that meeting, someone had compared my *"very spotted"* past to Graham's spotless record.

The implication was clear: *"You'll never be Billy Graham. This clearly isn't going to be your legacy. These things will follow you the rest of your life."*

Honestly, I'd never considered wanting to be like Billy Graham.

I'd never dreamed of stadiums and preaching to millions.
But if I had, that dream was now dead.

Now, the weight of my shame was paired with a hopeless future.

A life where any substantial ministry would be overshadowed by the paranoia of past sin. Something always lurking in the back corner, ready to come out and remind everyone that **I probably**

shouldn't be working for God.

I'd also like to interject here and say—I don't think the people in that meeting were purposefully trying to be hurtful. I think they were humans, thrown a giant curveball, just responding the best way they knew how in the moment.

To be fair, I gave them an army of curveballs.
A lot of people would've responded the same way.

But by divine leading or maybe just a lack of better options, we drove to North Carolina to visit Billy Graham's estate.

To keep my mind occupied, I started watching/reading interviews of people talking about what Graham had meant to them. One story came up that quite literally changed my life.

A well-known minister, who had publicly fallen decades earlier, shared about Graham's kindness toward him, at a time when all of his other friends had abandoned him.

He said he was in prison and no one would return his phone calls. Then one day, Graham showed up, gave him a big hug, and simply said, *"I am so sorry."*

That same man said the week he got out of prison, he was sitting in Billy Graham's house… eating fried chicken.

This is the most famous minister in the world we're talking about. Someone with a spotless reputation.

Hugging someone in jail.

After they'd abused their power in ministry.

The man wasn't trying to excuse what he'd done—far from it. But even in the face of all of that, Graham showed deep compassion. He didn't just say he was praying for him and move on. He stood in the middle of it with him.

As I finished reading that story, I whispered to myself, **"I can be THAT Billy Graham."**

I couldn't be the one who had never had skeletons in the closet. I couldn't be the one who played golf with presidents. But **I could be the one who finds the ostracized minister and offers hope.**

And from that moment on, the way I saw life and ministry changed drastically—**for the better.**

We can royally blow it in so many ways.
We can forget why we do what we do.

We can be the one who's talked down to. The one who sees the receipts for lavish ministry purchases. The one who's passed over. The one who never gets asked out to lunch.

We can also be the one who starts talking down to our fellow staff, the one who misuses the church credit card, expects special treatment, or becomes unapproachable.

Both sides of that same coin can leave us feeling like it's better to just get a *"normal job"* and love God on the weekends, like all the other *"normal people."*

We'll pray before board meetings, slap a fish logo on our store sign, and eat Chick-fil-A three times a week if we have to, just don't make us work for God again.

It's too hard. It asks too much.
And it doesn't pay enough.

It doesn't matter if you've seen flawless examples of ministry leaders or the absolute worst. It doesn't even matter if **you** have been that best or worst example.

"Ministry 101" is hope.

Hope that everything can change.

Hope that a new day is worth getting to and that **Jesus can redeem anyone and anything.**

In essence—**the tree can be saved.**

We often say, *"Church should be a hospital."* And while that's a beautiful concept, I'm not sure I fully agree.

Yes, it reminds us that our churches should be filled with hurt people looking to Jesus for healing. But a hospital isn't meant to be a place you stay. Its whole purpose is to fix you and get you out, to make room for more hurt people.

I'm not sure how well it would work for churches to adopt that exact same model.

I would, however, like to make this book a kind of hospital space for you.

Whether you feel like you have a ministry paper cut, or need full-on church-people brain surgery, I believe Jesus is on your side.

He is the most interested person in the world when it comes to seeing you not just serve His Father's house with honor, but grow in mental and emotional health while you do it.

So that you don't just work for God... you still love Him when you go home at night.

If you've ever met someone who's worked in ministry for fifty-plus years, it feels like seeing a unicorn. **You can't believe one actually exists.**

And if that person still **enjoys** ministry?
That's like seeing a unicorn with three heads!

Someone in their seventies who still cries when they talk about Jesus. Someone who still makes time to shake hands in the church lobby, even when they're clearly exhausted. I think we can all agree, that's a beautiful goal.

To go through life serving God and His people, with all the highs and lows that come with it, and somehow **make it to the other side with a tender heart and a hopeful soul.**

But that kind of life in ministry doesn't just happen.
It's fought for.

Paul said, "*I have fought the good fight, I have finished the race, I have kept the faith.*" *(2 Timothy 4:7)*

To finish a race, you have to not quit it.

Now, ministry has its costs. No denying that. Carrying the name of Jesus brings a certain weight. But it's a whole other thing to become delusional enough to carry His responsibilities.

Hopefully, we'll unpack more about how to avoid falling into that trap in the chapters ahead.

"Come to me, all who labor and are heavy laden, and I will give you rest. Take my yoke upon you and learn from me, for I am gentle and lowly in heart. You will find rest for your souls. For my yoke is easy, and my burden is light." (Matthew 11:28–30)

God is very good at being God.
He's had a lot of practice.

We're very good at being human.
We've had a lot of practice.

Thankfully, we serve the God who is the full embodiment of wisdom and patience—and He's on our side. So we have a lot to look forward to.

So here we go.

We're people who work for God, next to other people who also work for God.

There are personalities to maneuver, decisions to digest, potential to grow into, and all of it unfolding inside the greatest story the world has ever heard.

It **IS** an honor.
It can also be tricky at times.

But the good news is: **it is doable.**

You can survive working for God.

CHAPTER TWO

A TALE OF TWO TESTS

---

react vs. respond

The best part of being an adult has got to be that we're no longer forced to go to school.

I mean, can I get an amen!?

But as we enter the *"halls of ministry,"* we come into contact with many similar situations that feel a lot like starting a new school year.

We might get thrown into long-term relationships with people we don't know — thanks to random desk assignments (**aka, ministry teams**).

We're trying to figure out where the classrooms are, when lunch is, and even who the scariest teachers might be.

And once we start getting the lay of the land... it happens.

A test is given.

Our first chance to prove that we belong here.

Some schools give a test on day one, just to see where the students are starting from. Others wait a few weeks.

Either way, one thing stays the same:
Students take the test alone.

We're not competing with each other. The teacher doesn't interfere after it's handed out. Each student is graded based on their own interaction with the test.

It's a simple routine we all know.
But that's not how ministry works.

I'd like to propose something: **In ministry, there are always two different tests happening at the same time.**

The one you are taking.
And the one someone else is.

Now you might think — that's the same as school, right?

We're all in the same *"classroom,"* doing our own thing. We don't take each other's test. But here's the difference — in school, even though the tests are taken simultaneously, they're the same test.

Same questions. Same answers. Same grading rubric.
Ministry doesn't work like that.

Even when the circumstances are similar, **your test and their test might require different answers.**

Let me give you an example.

Let's say you step into a new role at a church.

The first three months? Glorious.

You're the golden child. Everyone's singing your praises, just for existing. You share ideas in staff meetings and people call you brilliant.

Your jokes are *"hilarious."*
Your songs are *"powerful."*
Your decisions are *"wise."*
Every interaction is *"a gift."*

Then suddenly... something shifts.

Like clockwork, on day one of month four, the winds change. Where you once felt like a shining star, you now feel... let's just say... less shiny.

You and another staff member bump into a disagreement. Nothing big, just a minor preference clash.

It probably starts with something like:
- *"What if we moved the piano to the other side of the stage?"*
- *"I was thinking we could switch out the youth camp speaker this year."*
- *"Maybe we let someone new do announcements this Sunday?"*

Innocent ideas. Right?

But sometimes these small suggestions act like tiny grenades.

You thought moving the piano would clean up the stage design. But you didn't know the worship leader's grandfather donated that piano 70 years ago.

You see an instrument.
They see legacy.

You want to give younger ministers more opportunities. But the youth pastor? They were saved under the ministry of the current youth camp speaker.

So your suggestion feels like an insult to their hero.

You see a faithful volunteer with a leadership gift and think: ***"They'd be great at Sunday announcements."*** But you didn't realize the current announcer is a beloved former staff member… whose family is quietly going through something heavy.

So your idea to ***"shake things up"*** feels like a lack of empathy for the very people who built the church you've just joined.

See the difference?

The space between your intentions and their perceptions can be as wide as the Grand Canyon.

And while you're still getting your bearings, that doesn't take away the anxiety of feeling like… **you're failing a test you didn't even know you were taking.**

That's a moment to pause.

To realize, **you're not the only one taking the test.**
The person you're interacting with is taking one, too.

We all know the Golden Rule: *"Do unto others as you would have them do unto you." (Matthew 7:12)*

But here's where we can go wrong. We assume we're only on the receiving end of things. That stuff just happens to us.

If we're not careful, we'll get trapped in this shallow mindset.

We'll trust our own intentions, but assume everyone else's motives.

That's a dangerous place to live.

So let's say you're in a moment of conflict.
First thing to remember?

God is watching this interaction.

Not in a judgmental way. But in a deeply invested, all-knowing kind of way. He sees the whole thing — the exchange, the internal responses — and He's watching you as an individual, too.

Your words.
Your tone.

Whether you're dismissive.
Whether you're kind, patient, and present.

This is where the real test shows up. **What does the overflow of your heart look like when you're pressed up against the wall?**

God doesn't grade your test based on someone else's performance.

So if you're thinking, **"Well, they had an attitude first, so I'm justified..."**, you're setting yourself up for disappointment and a longer learning curve.

As believers, our goal is to be a reflection of Jesus, not a mirror of circumstances **or the difficult people inside them.**

So here's the better approach: **Keep your eyes on your own test.**

God can handle the other test-takers.

Passing your test is the goal.
Not checking everyone else's answers.

MISLABELING ENEMIES

Now that we've addressed how important it is for you to take responsibility for your own test, I think it's important to highlight another kind of conflict that can show up, when others don't share the same philosophy of **test-taking etiquette.**

I once heard a story about a woman named Rebecca who had suffered a massive betrayal from her spouse.

She described how she was in a pit of emotional turmoil and felt like the enemy was laughing in her face through all of it.

One day, while praying and lamenting to the Lord about her circumstances, she admitted how angry it all had made her toward everyone involved.

She didn't know if she'd ever be able to move on from it.

Suddenly, she felt a tug in her heart.

A gentle voice nudged her, *"You've got your anger misplaced."*.

As she sat with that, her mind went to this scripture: *"For we do not wrestle against flesh and blood, but against principalities, against powers, against the rulers of the darkness of this age, against spiritual hosts of wickedness in the heavenly places." (Ephesians 6:12)*

Rebecca slowly began to realize **she had given the enemy a human face.**

She had taken the pain in her heart and used it as both a shield and a weapon, against other hearts.

Her real enemies weren't human at all.
What a revelation.

The people we have moments—or even seasons—of conflict with aren't villains.

Now, does that mean human beings can't cause deep harm with their words or actions?

Not even close.

But it does give us an opportunity to allow God to help us see them differently.

Keeping ourselves from mislabeling enemies is one small step in the right direction—**toward seeing people the way Jesus does.**

Remember, we serve a Savior who, in the midst of His greatest pain, betrayal, and mistreatment, still said from the cross: *"Father, forgive them; for they do not know what they're doing." (Luke 23:34)*

Jesus looked into angry, hateful eyes and still knew a greater reality.

So when moods shift, tempers flare, stress rises, or feelings get hurt, **let Jesus' words be where your emotions and imagination run back to.**

Because here's the truth: **We don't know anyone else's test-taking history.**

Who knows what kind of environment they were raised in?

Maybe one where people yelled during tests. Where they were insulted for not having the right answers. Where there were invisible bonus questions they didn't even know to look for.

And surviving in ministry?
That's not a new challenge.

People have been trying to find their own version of it for decades.

Sometimes that version looks... harsher.

"Toughen up. This is ministry, not Candyland!"

These are the moments when it's worth drawing a line in the sand between **reacting and responding.**

Imagine you get a call from a friend who's just run out of gas on the highway.

Your **reaction** might sound like, *"Oh no! Are you okay?"*.

You're concerned. You care.
That's great.

But if you were to **respond**, it would sound more like, *"Where are you? I'm on my way."*.

That's the difference.

Concern that moves into action.

You've probably heard the phrase, *"People don't care what you know until they know that you care."*.

We usually apply that to the work of ministry, but it matters just as much inside ministry.

When topics get sensitive or tension rises, how we react or respond can change everything.

Reacting tends to sound defensive:
- *"Why are you acting crazy?!"*
- *"How was I supposed to know that? No one told me!"*

Responding looks different.

You get your hands in the dirt.
You go the extra mile.

Back to one of our earlier examples— Say you want the piano

moved on stage.

Before you do, you make an announcement the Sunday before, giving people a heads-up that some things might look different. Then you go further.

You take time to honor the legacy that stage holds. You tell the story about how, seventy years ago, one man bought that piano for the church. How it's still being used today.

That's not manipulation.
That's not distraction.
That's honor.

You're still making the change, but now it's wrapped in care.

You're responding to sensitivity instead of reacting with defense.

Now I know what some of you might be thinking, *"This is the most dramatic and over-the-top scenario I've ever heard."*. If that's the case, then yeah, the example response probably feels over the top too.

It's just a piano, right?

- *"People don't really get bent out of shape over stuff like that."*
- *"Shouldn't we focus on important things like missions or ending homelessness?"*

I hear you.

And I'm not ignoring the *"silliness"* factor.

But here's the deal, churches are full of people.

Beautiful. Unique. Jesus-loving people... **with preferences.**

There's a reason why the entire congregation doesn't go to the same restaurant after church. Or why no one sits in the same pew.

From ages nine to ninety—People like what they like.

Businesses know this too. It's why most focus on one demographic at a time. Too many preferences, too much variety? It gets real hard to get anyone on the same page.

Ministry isn't any different.

So... do we just cater to every opinion and emotion that comes our way?

No.

Blind compliance isn't healthy for people or for teams. Ministry or not.

But I do believe that being a believer comes with a mandate that **we serve each other.**

I once heard a friend say, *"Most ministries don't need more leaders. They need more servants."*.

That instantly brought this scripture to mind: *"Whoever wants to be a leader among you must first be your servant." (Matthew 20:26)*

Jesus Himself says in Matthew 5:14: *"Whoever forces you to go one mile, go with them two."*

That was based on a law at the time.

If a Roman soldier asked you to carry something for one mile, you had to do it. Didn't matter how important your current task was. You dropped it, and you did what he said.

But then Jesus comes on the scene and tells us to go the extra mile. When you feel like you're being mistreated, **what can you do to keep your soul free?**

I heard a pastor once put it this way: *"Mile two is up to you."*

There are a lot of moments in working for God that **can feel more like work** than we'd prefer.

Navigating people — and all of their intricacies — can leave you feeling worn out.

But what if, in the face of their preferences, you chose to do more than what they're asking?

I know.

That's not always a small or easy thing to walk out. But just imagine what could happen as a result.

Revisiting the *"piano scandal"*...

What if your recommendation of honor and patience was met with people feeling touched — that you took time to celebrate people you've never met, and who aren't even alive anymore?

They may even feel, secretly, like those people were never truly honored while they were here — and now, someone's finally bringing healing to those feelings.

Suddenly, **we're getting insight into their sensitivity** about moving a piano in the first place.

And just like that, we're building bridges to their trust.

Who knows... maybe you'll want to move that piano again one day and this time, they'll barely make a fuss.

Because you're not here to have your way.
You're here to be part of the bigger picture.

The Bible is very clear:
The mercy you give is the mercy you get.

"Blessed are the merciful, for they will be shown mercy." (Matthew 5:7)

I've learned — in both good and not-so-good ways — that it's best to remember, your own humanity is capable of flaws.

So it only makes sense to show love and patience when someone else's humanity starts showing.

Drown people in mercy.
Because one day, you'll need to swim in it.

In short?
Pass your test.

CHAPTER THREE

LIGHT SWITCH THEORY

———

what's spiritual + what's practical

I want you to imagine I'm telling you a story about someone I'd describe as a bonafide genius.

Let's call them Dennis.

I've already laid some verbal groundwork — painted a vivid picture of how there's truly no one like him. And to prove it, I tell you I'm going to give an example of his brilliant daily life… something I've personally witnessed.

I say that I've seen him — on more than one occasion — walk into a dark room… and **turn on a light switch.**

There's no punch line.
No twist.

Not even an expensive light switch.

Just someone using a practical solution to a problem.

Naturally, your response would probably be underwhelmed. *"That's it? That doesn't even sound all that impressive. Everyone does that every day."*

But what if I added a little more context?

Not only does Dennis turn on the light switch, **he prays about it beforehand.** Sometimes he even calls in a couple of other people to discuss the pros and cons of turning the light on or leaving it off.

Feeling more impressed with him now?
Maybe.

But it's more likely that what you're actually feeling is confusion.

- "Wait... why are they praying about turning a light on?
- Is this a room in a church or in his house? And is there even a difference?
- Also... what is this story even about?"

I invited you into this little imagination exercise to open up a discussion around how we label things as *"spiritual"* or *"practical."*

Not just how we decide what's what, but how those labels influence the way we approach situations.

And even more, how they can add unnecessary stress.

I call this concept **Light Switch Theory** and it's easy to understand.

If something is as simple and obvious as turning on a light switch... it probably doesn't require a deeply

spiritual approach.

Some other *"light switch"* examples?
- Drinking water.
- Eating food.
- Trying not to die.

Most of these are just basic actions.
Common sense.

You don't need a prayer circle to decide if you should eat lunch. And most people would easily agree that not dying is a good idea. But have you ever tried to get a group of ministry workers to agree on a ministry decision?

Yeah. Not always as easy.

So how do we know what's a *"light switch"* and what's not?

Of course, *"not dying"* is a dramatic example. Ministry decisions are usually more nuanced. So a one-to-one comparison isn't fair.

But I think it helps to at least draw a big circle around the obvious ones — the things that are more *"light-switchy"* than others.

I've been part of a thousand worship services. Some five minutes long. Some four hours... no breaks. And no matter the length, they usually follow a similar rhythm. That rhythm includes something called a soundcheck.

If you don't know what that is, the name does most of the work for you: It's a time for everyone on stage, and behind the soundboard, to make sure mics and instruments are working properly.

It also gives the band and vocalists a chance to rehearse before service starts.

The overall goal?

Get on the same page.
Avoid distractions.

Create a smooth experience for people to engage in worship.

Because if you've ever been in the middle of a song and heard a guitar in the wrong key... or a mic cut out... you know just how distracting those moments can be.

Soundchecks help reduce that.

But in the moment, it doesn't always feel like help. Sometimes it slips into tension. **And tension... opens the door to stress.**

And stress?

It brings its own soundtrack:
- rushed words
- short tones
- unspoken judgments

Not exactly the ideal atmosphere for leading others in worship.

Philippians 4:6–7 says: *"Do not be anxious about anything, but in every situation, by prayer and petition, with thanksgiving, present your requests to God. And the peace of God, which transcends all understanding, will guard your hearts and your minds in Christ Jesus."*

But let's be honest, what actually causes the stress?

Maybe someone didn't learn the song beforehand — now the team is scrambling.

Maybe a singer forgot the lyrics — and everyone's looking around, confused.

Maybe there's a tech issue — no one's fault — but it's eating up time and patience.

And maybe… **patience is in short supply.**

Maybe a band member is frustrated because someone else didn't prepare.

Maybe a leader feels like they've had the same tech issue five weeks in a row and no one's fixing it.

**Stress doesn't ask permission. It just shows up.
And worse — it's contagious.**

Sometimes you're not stressed because you're stressed…
You're stressed because they're stressed.

So what do we do?

Can we prevent people from feeling stress in the first place?
That would be the dream, wouldn't it?

But even in the healthiest teams and holiest rooms… people are still going to be people. Still, I do think there's a way to **take some of the sting out of it.** Maybe even cut it in half.

Here's where **Light Switch Theory** comes in.

We start by getting really good at spotting the *"light switch"* decisions. The things we don't need to overthink or over-spiritualize.

For example:
- We don't need to pray about having batteries in the mic.
- We don't need to pray about playing a song in the right key or with the correct chords.
- We don't need to pray about whether or not we should sing the song the pastor asked for.

All of that?
Light switches.

They're actions that simply need to be done — not soul-searching moments about the heart behind the action.

And if that last line made you tilt your head a little — maybe even feel slightly suspicious — let me explain...

I love hearing stories from ministers — their experiences in different environments over the years, the consistencies they've noticed, and the differences they've had to navigate.

One, in particular, always stuck with me.

A worship leader named Ben had just joined a church staff and was being deeply impacted by a specific worship music movement at the time. He started leading songs from that movement every week, and the people seemed to respond really well.

All was right in the world.

Then one day, a traveling evangelist named John came into town to preach a series of meetings. John had a rhythm to his gatherings.

He typically ended his sermons with a time of singing and prayer.

Ben, without discussing anything with John, just kept doing what had been working. Same songs. Same flow.

After a service one night, John pulled Ben aside.

"I really love what you're doing," he said. *"But I'm noticing a lot of these songs are pretty slow... and I think they might be making people a little sleepy and disconnected. Is it possible to add some more up-tempo songs?"*

He explained that people were showing up tired after work and sitting through long services — he just wanted to help keep them engaged.

Let's just say... **Ben did not respond well.**

He unleashed. Accused John of trying to manipulate emotions instead of letting the Spirit move. Then he stormed off and drove home in a rage, stewing over the nerve of the guy.

But that night, **sleep didn't come easy.**

No matter how much Ben tried to feel justified, he couldn't shake the weight of conviction. Something in him knew he had handled it wrong.

The next morning, disheveled and exhausted, Ben went straight to John. *"God won't leave me alone about this. I need to apologize. If you want faster songs, I'll give you a hundred of them, in every key I can sing!"*

They talked it out. Together, they found a rhythm that worked for both of them — one that truly helped people engage during those services.

Ben tasted the bitterness of demanding his own way... but also the relief of surrendering to someone else's vision.

**That shift didn't change who he was.
It changed how he served.**

Ben wasn't becoming someone different because of a leader's request, **he was adjusting his personal vision in order to honor someone else's.**

That's a major difference.

That shift leads to wide open spaces — places where you can grow, thrive, and yes, even survive in ministry for decades to come.

"Whatever you do, work at it with all your heart, as working for the Lord, not for human masters... It is the Lord Christ you are serving."
— *Colossians 3:23–24*

**We need to remember: God is our boss.
But He cares about how we treat our co-workers too.**

In ministry, we sit in a lot of **metaphorical seats.**

One day, we're leading a small group. The next, we're scrubbing floors after an outreach. One moment, we're guiding others in worship... Then we're being asked to defer to a leader's direction.

The roles shift.
The seat changes.

And when we're honest... sometimes we just want to pick the seat ourselves.

We start saying things like:
- *"Why can't the pastor just let me sing what I want?"*
- *"Don't they trust me?"*
- *"God doesn't care about this kind of decision. He cares about the people."*

That's what I call **heart talk.**

It's when we dress up a complaint in spiritual language and say, *"I'm just sharing my heart."* But a lot of times, that's just a churchy way of saying, *"I think you're an idiot."*

It's sneaky. It feels holy.

But it's actually heading into dangerous territory... **Absalom territory.**

Absalom was King David's son.
And he was really good at looking like he cared.

The Bible says he would meet people who didn't get what they wanted from the king, and he'd say things like, *"You've got a strong case! It's too bad no one will hear it... If I were in charge, you'd get justice." (See 2 Samuel 15:3)*

He sounded like a man of the people, but he was really just building a throne for himself.

So here's the thing: **It's not evil to believe you're capable. It IS dangerous to assume you're the perfect fit for every seat.**

You might have preferences — that's normal.

But when preferences turn into barriers, you start blocking the very connections God wants you to build.

"Let us therefore make every effort to do what leads to peace and to mutual edification." — Romans 14:19

So what do we do when someone wants to *"share their heart"*? Shouldn't we respect that?

Sure. Sometimes.

But here's the filter: Are they offering a spiritual insight on a spiritual matter? Or are we over-spiritualizing something as simple as turning on a light switch?

Not every decision needs a prayer meeting.
Not every opinion needs a microphone.

Sometimes, serving another's vision isn't about giving up yours. It's about becoming someone who can co-exist and co-lead — **without becoming an obstacle.** And that's the kind of person who goes the distance.

WHAT TO DO NEXT

Now, if you look around and notice that something is indeed a *"light switch"*, and it's not being approached appropriately, then you've got some choices to make.

First:
- Are you the main leader in the room?
- Are you leading alongside someone else?
- Or are you not in charge at all in that scenario?

Depending on where you land, that answer will help you decide how to respond respectfully.

Second, it's helpful to remember: **prevention is typically better than restoration.**

Assuming a microphone will need new batteries and making sure it's done before someone needs it to speak is probably better than it turning off mid-sentence and triggering a full-blown scramble by a stressed-out production team.

That kind of moment can lead to finger-pointing, blame-shifting, and lots of heat about who was responsible... Not enjoyable.

Third: prep yourself for patience.

If we're not careful, we'll get so desperate for change that we try to do too much, too quickly.

Just because you notice something that's off — and can see how it should be better — doesn't mean everyone else is going to feel less stressed right away.

But I believe **small ripples create big waves.**
And **clarity can create unity.**

Sometimes clarity sounds like someone standing up and saying, *"We're not going to approach a microphone like we do a sermon. One carries a message. The other amplifies that message. Both are valuable, but both are different. And that's okay."*

What about the other things that are **NOT** light switches?

- The songs the worship team chooses to sing.
- How we handle a meeting with staff members we disagree with.
- Even what we plan to preach or say on that mic *(now that it has fresh batteries)*.

These are not implied or automatic.
They grow. They adapt. Week to week. Year to year.

They shift based on what you and your team feel like God is leading you to sing or say, for your local community of believers.

There are areas of ministry where we hold common sense in one hand and faith in the other.

And there are moments we're not sure which hand to grip tighter.

- Believing for a loved one to be saved.
- Trusting God to miraculously pay a bill.
- Or even asking Him to use us for something bigger than ourselves.

These are the kinds of places where **common sense doesn't always feel like the most trustworthy counselor.**

We won't always agree on what should be considered a light switch. But we'll find more common ground than we realize.

The more we agree on, the less stress we carry.

Some studies suggest that **a person has only so much decision-mak**

ing capacity each day. As the day goes on, that capacity fades. You make your best decisions in the morning... and your worst ones at night.

Does that feel accurate in your own life?

I think the same can be said for our capacity to take a spiritual approach to things.

Now, as Christians, we understand that life is always spiritual — we're sons and daughters of God.

But I mean something else.

I mean the difference between spiritual paranoia and a spiritual lens.

One makes you feel stressed.
The other anchors your perspective.

If everything is always spiritual, then everything will always feel like it carries eternal weight. And anyone who thinks like that long enough is going to be properly stressed.

But what if... in the middle of the moment... you could pause, breathe, and realize: **Maybe I'm just sweating over batteries.**

Light switches matter.
But not more than the things they're shining a light on.

And definitely not more than the people flipping the switches.

CHAPTER FOUR

BOUNDARIES vs. WALLS

———

healthy balances + distinctions

In the past few years, I've seen a surge of discussions around boundaries in ministry — where they've been absent, mishandled, or even resented.

Maybe those conversations have always existed, but to me, they've definitely become more visible.

So where has this surge come from?

I'd suggest it's largely been spearheaded by **wounded, grown-up pastor's kids.**

Going back to my own experience as a *"PK,"* I had a very specific view of ministry boundaries as a child — mostly that there weren't any.

I'm an observer by nature, even from a young age.

So much of what I learned wasn't taught to me directly. It was picked up in the background, through the behavior of the adults around me.

I don't think that communication was always intentional, but it still left an impact.

One of the first things I noticed?
People always get first place.

Seems noble, right?

But here's the catch: those people aren't always your family. And those people aren't always you. **Their needs often came before your own.**

Try explaining that to a seven-year-old.

It wasn't unusual for our family to be home on a Thursday night, relaxing, only for everything to shift into *"ministry mode"* because of a phone call — someone needing a hospital visit, counseling, or some kind of emergency support.

I saw the fatigue that came from that kind of constant availability.

But I also saw something else: **the deep gratitude from the people we served.** And even more, I saw how grateful my family was to serve the people of God in any way they could.

It wasn't just a job for them.
It was a high calling.

One they'd probably blush at even thinking about complaining over.

But again... I was a child.

And no one felt responsible for helping me understand why our life was our own—until it wasn't.

So I did what a lot of kids do.
I observed. And I assumed.

And when you assume long enough without answers, you end up creating your own.

So as much as I saw both sides of the coin, it was hard not to land on this one simple belief: **People who make themselves available are people who care.**

Which meant... people who **DON'T** make themselves available must **NOT** care.

Now, no one wants to be known as the person who doesn't care. So naturally, I began to see any sacrifice in my family's boundaries as **a badge of honor.** Never even considered that it could sometimes be unhealthy or unwise.

And here's where our ministry minds love to jump in and argue:
- *"Jesus didn't draw boundaries between Himself and people."*
- *"We didn't get into ministry for a life of comfort."*
- *"Jesus gave His life for us, surely we can give Him our time."*

I get it. I do.

And honestly, I agree with so much of that.

But... there's a difference between a boundary and a wall.

And I think sometimes, we don't always know **how to tell the two apart.**

I would define a boundary as a **parameter.**

Let's say you own a house.

The land your house sits on has parameters that separate it from other people's property. You can typically cross those boundary lines with little effort, but once you've crossed them, you've stepped into an area that belongs to someone else.

It's rarely an actual line painted on the grass. It's documented on a map — one you can look at to see where **your land ends and where someone else's begins.**

A wall, however, is something I would define as an **obstacle.**

It's something you have to put effort into climbing over.

If that same house was surrounded by walls instead of boundaries, crossing from one side to the other would become a lot more difficult.

A wall keeps people out — and keeps others in.

I believe walls are created where boundaries aren't stewarded.

Now, when I say stewarded, that could mean:
- communicated
- kept consistent
- enforced with kindness

Think about it.

Why would someone build a wall around their property?

One can naturally assume the owners were either paranoid about people not respecting their boundaries... or their parameters had been crossed so many times they finally decided enough was enough.

"If people won't honor my parameters, then I'll create an obstacle that prevents any further interaction."

Are you starting to catch the nuance?

I'll never forget the day I experienced this reality in my own ministry story.

I had joined a staff of friendly, hard-working, gospel-card-carrying people. Many had been there for years because they so deeply believed in the mission.

You couldn't help but let the inspiration rub off on you.

It was a church that was healthy in its size and reputation. But this type of *"external health"* often creates a high standard for executing events and conferences throughout the year.

One event in particular was coming up.
My first *"big one"* while on staff.

We had a large meeting with everyone involved to make sure no nuts or bolts had slipped through the cracks before final prep kicked in.

A leader gave us a charge for the hours and days ahead.

A coach-type speech — the kind that reminds you not just of what you're doing, but *why you're doing it.*

Then they wrapped it with this statement: ***"Remember, we don't have to do this... we get to do this."***

I immediately thought to myself, Wow. What a great line!

I'd never heard that in a church context before, and I was anxious to put it to work.

The event went off without a hitch.

Lives were changed. We were tired.
A good kind of tired, but still tired.

As was typical after big events, the staff would get some time off to compensate for all the overtime. But this time, many of us were asked to do additional things that would cut into that rest.

Not because it was urgent, just because it was preferred by a few leaders.

Now, I'm all for being a team player. I'll do what needs to be done. But in this case, it felt like we were being taken advantage of a little.

I tossed out a few light concerns.

Not full-on confrontation. Just giving them a chance to do what was right without directly calling out what felt wrong.

I wasn't trying to dodge responsibility, I just wanted them to consider how tired we were... and **whether the extra requests really required the urgency they were pushing.**

And very quickly, that same line was laid back on the table: *"We don't have to do this... we get to do this."*

But this time, it didn't hit the same.

It didn't feel inspiring.
It felt... off.

Like maybe that line wasn't just motivational.

Maybe it was also a tool — used occasionally to make us feel bad and keep us compliant.

Whatever the case was, I smiled and did it anyway. I didn't want to look like a troublemaker at my first major event.

"It's not that big of a deal," I thought. *"This is an honor. And think of all the amazing things God just did — that's what really matters."*

So I moved on.
For the glory of God, of course.

More events came and went.
About a year later, I noticed something.

I started making sure I was *"busy"* during certain points of events.

Why?

Because it gave me cover.

Cover from not-so-surprising surprise extra work requests.
Cover from awkward confrontation.
Cover from that gut feeling of being used.

I figured it would keep me under the radar.

Until one day, an office disagreement uncovered someone's issue with me.

They called out the fact that I hadn't done the same extra work they had been asked to do. And in my unresolved frustration, the *"good impression"* gloves came off.

I snapped.

I unloaded about how they didn't respect my boundaries. How they used *"get to"* statements to manipulate. How just because they didn't have boundaries didn't mean I wasn't allowed to have any.

I was unrelenting.

But as the argument came to a close... it became painfully obvious: **I no longer had boundaries. I had built walls.**

I had created concrete obstacles between me and another teammate **— all because I hadn't been brave enough to steward parameters around my personal time.**

And this was the result.

Ephesians 4:2-3 says: *"Be completely humble and gentle; be patient, bearing with one another in love. Make every effort to keep the unity of the Spirit through the bond of peace."*

Even though it wasn't my intention, my *"bear with one another"* energy had run out.

And I had no one to blame but myself.

I hadn't drawn the line.
So I built the wall.

There's a distinction we all need to recognize if we want longevity in ministry: **We can't punish people with walls when they don't realize they're crossing our boundaries.**

Imagine this...

You go to your next-door neighbor's house every Saturday.

You exchange some friendly conversation and genuinely enjoy it. You've done it for so long now that you've forgotten many of the practical steps it took to build that comfort in the beginning.

At first, you'd knock and wait outside. Eventually, you just let yourself in with a warm, *"Hello!"* You also used to listen more carefully — cautious not to overstep. But now? If something is said out loud, you feel like you have full permission to jump in with advice.

Then one Saturday, you show up like always... Only this time, there's an iron gate with a lock on it. You can't even reach the front door.

Assuming your neighbor forgot what day it is, you call out, *"Hey, neighbor! It's me! I can't get in!"*

But no one comes out.

It happens again the next week. And the next. Until one day, you finally catch your neighbor getting into their car.

This is your chance.

Surely they didn't know you were out there each week. Maybe they thought you stopped coming.

You approach them quickly, ready to clear the air...
But the look on their face — it says everything.

Before long, the painful gaps start filling in. They tell you the gate was intentionally built to keep you out. They explain how your unannounced entries and constant advice became overwhelming.

How they didn't want to hurt your feelings... How they needed space but didn't know how to ask for it... How they're bad at saying *"no"* — so instead they waited too long, got desperate, and hoped a gate would fix what they couldn't communicate.

How would that make you feel?

Probably hurt. Maybe even betrayed.
And definitely confused.

How were you supposed to know they felt that way?

If you'd known where their boundaries were, you could've adjusted. You might not have agreed with their preferences, but at least you'd have had the chance to respond with patience and grace.

That's what we're trying to prevent.

Let's give people clarity on our parameters, so they can give grace

in their approach.

"Simply let your 'yes' be 'yes,' and your 'no,' 'no'…" — *Matthew 5:37*

If not, we risk punishing people with relational obstacles… just because they couldn't read our minds.

IMAGINARY CONCRETE

Now that we've talked about the difference between boundaries and walls, there's one more layer to look at: **our imagination.**

It's not just about having honest conversations.

It's about being honest with ourselves — especially with what's going on internally.

Proverbs 18:11 says, *"A rich man's wealth is his strong city, and like a high wall in his imagination."*

Let that sink in.

It's possible to have a wall in our imagination that prevents us from seeing the world clearly.

Not just a barrier — but something we can't see over.

I believe that wall has a name: **familiar.**

In this verse, the wall is wealth. The man is so used to abundance that he can no longer imagine life without it. That doesn't just lead to personality pitfalls, it creates hurdles in empathy and connection.

So, what are you familiar with?

What thoughts or beliefs have lived with you so long that you've stopped questioning them?

They might not even be *"bad"* things.

But if they dull your vision or make your ministry less effective — they deserve a closer look.

I'm not asking you to become overly critical. I'm reminding you that **familiarity isn't always harmless.** Especially when it comes to people.

Remember the frustrated neighbor?

The real issue wasn't just the iron gate.
It was the unchecked familiarity with their space.

When we're around people long enough, we can get lazy in our understanding.

We stop asking questions.
We start assuming intentions.
We misread cues or ignore subtle shifts.

And that's how walls start getting built — **without a single word ever being spoken.**

There might not be obvious boundaries on the outside... But inwardly, the distance grows.

People are talking, but they're not building relationship.

Boundaries draw lines. Walls create distance.

I've seen people grow close to a pastor, forget they're talking to a leader, push too far with a joke — and lose trust in the relationship.

On the flip side, I've seen parents skip their kid's baseball games because they believed God would be disappointed if they chose a *"frivolous"* event over ministry.

If you're anything like me, this tension always feels present.

Because it's true: we're not called to just *"do whatever we want."* Our lives aren't our own.

But — and this is important — I believe God also invites us to tear down the walls in our imagination that say:
- *"This is ministry-worthy."*
- *"This is not."*

Emotional and relational walls might be invisible... **But that doesn't mean they're not felt.**

Let's allow that obviousness to push us toward honesty. Because if we're honest about where we lack healthy boundaries, we're already one step closer to tearing down those walls.

Even better — we can stop new ones from being built in the first place.

Fewer walls mean more people can reach us.

And being reachable is a healthy way to be available.

Now — will everyone love your new passion for drawing lines? Maybe not.

But what will they get that they didn't have before?

Someone who truly believes they *"get to"* do ministry.

Not as a trendy slogan... but as **a personal heartbeat.**

CHAPTER FIVE

COAT OF MANY PROMISES

---

potential with patience

One of the most famous characters in the entire Bible isn't a person — **it's a coat.**

Joseph's coat of many colors, to be exact.

It's likely the **most famous piece of clothing in human history.**

People who've never heard John 3:16 still know about that garment.

I've seen paintings, musicals, cartoons, felt boards — you name it — all trying to capture the public's fascination with this patchwork of fabric for as long as I can remember.

But why do we care so much about it? What draws us to it? **Do we even know?**

I don't think we can put it in proper perspective without also considering the person who wore it.

Joseph's story has become synonymous with trust, grace, and forgiveness.

He was betrayed by his brothers, sold into slavery, falsely accused of rape, imprisoned, and forgotten by the very people he helped — only to be used by God to save an entire nation from starvation and extinction.

And yet... for all that drama and redemption, we still often linger around the coat he wore for just a few verses.

Curious, isn't it?

I mean, I've seen some cool coats — **but come on.**

If we're going to examine this coat, we need to look at where Joseph was in life when he first put it on.

"Now Israel loved Joseph more than any of his other sons, because he had been born to him in his old age; and he made an ornate robe for him. When his brothers saw that their father loved him more than any of them, they hated him and could not speak a kind word to him. Joseph had a dream, and when he told it to his brothers, they hated him all the more." (Genesis 37:3-5)

Whew. So much to unpack in just three sentences.

We have someone who is both deeply loved and deeply hated at the same time.

The love comes from genuine affection.

The hate? **A direct reaction to that affection.**

His father sees something in Joseph — potential, promise, proof of God's faithfulness.

And he wants everyone else to see it too.

So, he gives Joseph a coat to make it clear: **"When you see my son, I want you to see what I see, someone destined for amazing things."**

But imagine what a spectacle Joseph must've looked like in it.

How many people misread that coat of affection as a badge of arrogance?

I'm sure folks passed him on the road and muttered, **"Wow... he must really think he's something."**

In that light, the jealousy of his brothers starts to make more sense.

In ministry, we have a social currency called **"humility."**

We might not say it out loud, but if we see a pastor working two jobs just to volunteer at church, we think — now that's humility.

On the flip side, a pastor with a healthy salary?

Well, some might secretly wonder if they've drifted too far from the trenches.

So how would we rate the humility of Joseph and his flashy coat?

We know how the story ends, which gives us perspective.

But what if we didn't?

Imagine someone rolls into your city driving a brand new, brightly colored car.

You ask them where they got it, and they say, *"My dad got it for me... because he loves me."*

Yeah...

We all know exactly what we'd think.

And it probably wouldn't be, *"Wow, God must have a mighty plan for their life."*

More likely?

"Wow, God — I'm so sorry You have to deal with people like that."

Why?

Because judging a book by its cover is easy.

Are we right in our judgment? Who knows. Most of the time, we never intend on reading that book in the first place.

But what about our own coats of promise?

What about all the encouraging words, the late-night conversations, the dreams and declarations we've collected over time?

How do we "wear" the things God has spoken over our lives?

When we're just starting in ministry, the road ahead feels wide open — anything is possible.

We haven't burned out yet.
We don't need a sabbatical.

Elder meetings still sound exciting.

We could do church all day, every day — and love it.

And when others see us at that stage, they start to cast their vision on us too.

A spiritual father might say, *"I see you becoming a powerful worship leader one day."*

A mentor might declare, *"You've got the heart of a future executive pastor."*

They may not hand us literal coats — but if they say those things often enough and loud enough, people will see us wearing them just the same.

And this is where Joseph's story comes in.

First: Joseph is loved by his father. And we are loved by our Father.

"We love Him because He first loved us." (1 John 4:19)

God has knit us together with gifts, passions, personalities, and purpose. He wants to express Himself through us.

What an incredible honor.

His kindness covers us. We walk in mercy and grace every single day. The Bible says we didn't earn any of this. **Even our ability to walk it out is a gift.**

So if God gives you a coat — **it's not because you've proven you know how to wear it.** It's because He thinks you look good in His love.

Second: Joseph's brothers weren't mad at the coat... They were mad at what it meant.

Their father's love for Joseph made them feel unloved.
It wasn't about fabric, it was about favor.

They believed, *"If Dad gave him that... then we must've missed out."*

And we do this too.

We start thinking God only has so much to go around.

Someone else's voice, success, influence, favor — starts to feel like evidence that God skipped over us.

We don't want to feel envy.
But we do.

And it's easy to forget: **We have our own coats too.**
And there's no rule that says they all have to look the same.

Third: Joseph had a dream... and felt safe enough to share it.

Why?

Because his father's love gave him permission to be who he truly was.

I wonder if he'd had dreams before, but brushed them off.

"Eh, maybe it was just something I ate..."

But maybe one day, he woke up from a dream... pulled on that new coat... and had a moment of clarity: *"Wait a minute... My dad gave me this amazing coat. Maybe... just maybe... he really sees something in me. And maybe it's okay if I start to see it too."*

So to recap:
- Joseph's father covered him with a noticeable gift of his love.
- Those who should've celebrated became frustrated.
- And Joseph simply came into agreement with what his father thought about him.

These things kick-start a perfect storm of pain and suffering for Joseph for several years to come.

All of this... because of a stupid jacket!

I want you to think about all of the wonderful things you believe are ahead of you in ministry.

Even if you've never had anyone personally say how God wanted to use you, it's highly likely you've allowed yourself to daydream — about the many ways your life could make an impact, big or small, for the honor of the name of Jesus.

Let me be clear: **A dream for God to take your life and do some thing with it is not evil.**

Now, if your goal is to manipulate emotions for financial gain, politically rub shoulders for power, and then sprinkle some *"Jesus"* on top of it... you might want to consider a different career.

But most likely, **that's not who you are.**

You're someone who loves God and just wants to serve Him, in whatever way you feel He's called you to.

That's a wonderful heart posture to start from.

It may not be a literal coat you wear, but God has clothed you with a recognizable gift of His love.

Maybe you have a gift to teach. A voice to sing. An ability to relate to people. Even a mind for mathematics.

Sure, you may have been born with some of it.
Maybe you've worked hard to refine it.

But the root system underneath it all is still God.

Some people will see those invisible coats, and instead of celebrating them, they'll envy you.

That envy often leads to tension.

And whether they realize it or not, it usually doesn't start with you. It's about their frustration with God.

If they truly believed what He gave them was enough... they wouldn't be so bothered by what He gave you.

I once heard a minister tell a story about their friend releasing a book.

They noticed their initial thought was, *"Big deal. I could write a book. I'd probably write a better book than them anyway. I've heard them talk, and if their book sounds anything like the way they talk... I bet no one will like it."*

But within moments, they felt so convicted by their attitude that they shifted to something completely different: *"Wow, that's amazing! I can't believe they wrote a book. I've always wanted to write a book but never made it happen. What amazing follow-through they have! I want to be more like that. People seem to really like them — I bet their book will do really well."*

That shift says everything.

One thought-process is drenched in the belief that God is stingy, and you better get what you can before someone else does.

The other is grounded in truth: **God is good to them AND to you.**

That story has always been a perfect reminder for me.

Someone else's vibrant coat doesn't have to feel like an insult to mine.

And that realization?
It can truly keep you from going crazy.

PERMISSION TO BE YOU

There is another area of Joseph's coat scenario that's a little trickier: How we come into agreement with what God says about us — and how that approach affects our relationships with others.

In ministry, I often see people lean on the *"haters gonna hate"* mindset.

And frankly... I wouldn't recommend it.

I get the sentiment.
People should focus on their own lives.

And often, their critiques come from jealousy, not godly concern.

And yes — there's real power in the confidence that comes from knowing who you are in Christ and what He's called you to do.

But...

Sometimes people confuse their gift as THE gift.

They don't just think they're a great worship leader — **they believe they're the only one who should ever lead worship.**

Or they don't just believe they have a word from God — **they believe they're the only one in the room who can hear Him accurately.**

I was once at a ministry with an incredible worship leader on staff.

Yes, they had a great voice. But beyond that, the room just naturally unified when they sang. So, many of the leaders depended heavily on them — because they knew what they'd consistently get:

A voice they loved.
And a unified room.

Sounds amazing, right?

Well, as the ministry grew, more and more gifted worship leaders became available, and wanted the opportunity to serve.

Many ministries would dream of such a *"problem."*

But those new worship leaders weren't given any real opportunities.

Why?

Because giving someone else a chance meant:
- The possibility of not loving their voice as much
- The room taking longer to unify
- Having to adjust to a different personality or style

Those small risks felt too big.
Momentum mattered more.

So preferences took precedence over possibility.

The leaders' affection for one worship leader's gift turned into their preference for all worship leaders.

So if you wanted to get a shot at leading worship there, you learned pretty quickly: **Morph into what they already like... or don't bother.**

If everyone does the same thing, then no one rocks the boat. And no one gets in trouble for doing something the leaders don't prefer.

Those *"up-and-comers"*?
They were learning how to put on *"goat's hair."*

Yes, you read that correctly — goat's hair.

The Bible tells the story of a man named Jacob who wanted a blessing from his father so badly... he impersonated his brother Esau to get it.

Esau and Jacob were twins, but they were built very differently.

Esau was the firstborn — a natural outdoorsman, rugged, and extremely hairy.

Jacob was the second — preferred to be indoors, and had smooth skin.

You'd assume it wouldn't be too hard to tell the two apart.
Except... their father had gone blind in his old age.

So Jacob's mother came up with a plan.

She decided they'd trick the father into thinking Jacob was Esau, for the sake of getting a Jacob a blessing that didn't belong to him.

Genesis 27:16 says, *"She covered Jacob's arms and the smooth part of his neck with the skin of the young goats."*

Jacob literally changed his external appearance, because he thought that was the only way to move forward in life.

And the wild part?
It worked.

The trick paid off.

They got what they wanted, but not without wrecking the family in the process *(as you can imagine)*.

We don't arrive in ministry as flawless, finished products.

There's so much we have to learn...
So much to grow into.

But if we're not careful, our impatience along the way will tempt us to pretend our way to "success."

And that's the dangerous part — **pretending might actually work.**

You might get the role.
The opportunity.
The title.

But if you have to wear someone else's coat to get there, **you'll still be you when you arrive.**

And that version of you will be tired, confused, and disoriented.
So keeping your heart in honest patience is vital.

Let yourself grow in the areas you didn't expect to blossom.

And just as important — **let yourself agree with what God has already placed on your life.**

We need to honor other people's gifts.

But we also need to feel permission to enjoy the coat our Father made for us to wear.

It fits perfectly — **even if we don't feel like we earned it.**

"There are different kinds of gifts, but the same Spirit distributes them. There are different kinds of service, but the same Lord. There are different kinds of working, but in all of them and in everyone, it is the same God at work." (1 Corinthians 12:4–6)

Every *"coat"* around you has a backstory.
A journey. A process.

God gave those gifts to people because He loves them — **and those gifts are a strength to you, not a threat.**

Joseph's moment in the coat was short.
But his story was long.

We see God's promises and often expect them to arrive early in our ministry years. But like Joseph, our story stretches across decades, not just initial seasons.

Victories.
Setbacks.
Tests.
Breakthroughs.

Fabric might rip — but love endures.

And if we can stay anchored... Not just in the coat... But in the love the coat represents — it becomes easier to carry the endurance that pushed Joseph from pit to palace.

So take a breath.
Stand tall.

And remember: **You look good in His love.**

CHAPTER SIX

THE RED CHAIR EFFECT

---

stewarding loyalty

Who's your favorite leader of all time?

Maybe someone you've only read about. Or someone you've been close to for years. Maybe someone you just met, or even your kindergarten teacher. *(Shout out to Mrs. Bagwell.)*

Now that you're picturing that leader in your mind, think about this: **How much would you trust their judgment if they gave you advice on something important?**

Would you follow it all the way?
Halfway?

There's something powerful about having **a voice in your life you really trust.**

If you're facing a big decision or walking through uncharted terri tory, a wise voice of counsel is like pure gold.

It's not just about having someone willing to pour into your life—
it's about someone who sees who you are and wants to help you
uncover **what you could become.**

When you find that kind of person, you realize just how long you
went without it.

I had a leader like that—Dr. David Horton.

I'd admired him from afar for years, but got the chance for a real
relationship with him for two short years before he passed.

In that time, I learned so much, from his insights on ministry, to
the importance of personal devotion, to how to serve local churches with different visions. He even helped me give God room to
redefine what *"success"* meant for me.

Dr. Horton's impact was so deep that I naturally formed a loyalty
to him.

I wasn't alone—many others were forever changed by his heart and
example.

He loved his spouse fiercely, was honest about his struggles, and
anchored our anxious questions about the future in the hope of
Jesus and His Word.

When he passed, he left behind a legacy of trusting God through
all of life's mysteries, even if that meant bringing honest complaints
instead of hypocritical praise.

I think we can all agree:

Being loyal to someone like that feels right.

One day I was talking with a friend, Tom, who also served under Dr. Horton.

He shared an analogy about loyalty that I'll never forget.

We were discussing ministry leaders—who inspired us, who we wanted to learn from—when Tom said this about serving under Dr. Horton: *"If Dr. Horton walked into a room and pointed at a black chair, saying it was red, someone might correct him: 'No, that chair's black, not red.' But if I heard him say that chair was red, I wouldn't correct him. <u>I'd just paint the chair red.</u>"*

The moment he said that I felt this rush of what I can only describe as *"pumped loyalty."*

"That's exactly how it should be!" I told him. *"We should have our leaders' backs no matter what. If this ship goes down, we're all going down with it."*

How loyal do I sound?

Too loyal? Just right?

Maybe teetering on cult-like?

I call this the **red chair effect.**

It's a mindset where your mouth says "yes" before your brain even asks "why."

Where you adjust to whatever your leader says or does—**without asking if you should.**

But where does this come from?

If a leader truly impacts our lives, shows strong character, and bears real fruit, we often respond with extreme gratitude.

Maybe they helped us through a tough financial season. Or gave us a shot when no one else would. Maybe they gently reminded us that *"arrival"* isn't the same as being noticed by others.

But how do we show that gratitude?
Often, **through loyalty.**

We might not be able to pay them back or open doors for them, but we can be loyal.

When they share an idea, our loyalty shines through in our flawless commitment.

Even if our hearts are in the right place, this kind of loyalty isn't always healthy—or fully warranted.

Even the best leaders aren't perfect, and it's important to ask: **Where is my loyalty coming from? And how do I communicate it?**

If it's rooted in gratitude for what leaders have done for you, remember—other people may not share the same experience.

Someone might have never even heard of them before.

When we catch ourselves getting defensive or angry at criticism—saying, *"They're amazing! You don't know what they've been through!"*—we might be right.

But that doesn't mean those other experiences are wrong.

It just means our gratitude-based loyalty might look delusional from other perspectives.

So how do we handle this middle ground?

I say: **build a bridge.**

"Middle ground" implies that there is a gap between two sides, but we don't need something to erase that gap, as much as we need something to provide transportation from one side to the other.

That's where a bridge comes in.
Specifically a relational one.

A bridge gives us a safe way to travel back and forth between different opinions and experiences.

We can honor those above us while listening to those around us, even when they don't agree.

In short, you don't need to be a leader's ambassador.

You're a child of God first.

HONORING SMART

Now, what if you're reading this chapter so far and thinking, *"I don't know if I feel particularly loyal to any leader. Is that bad?"*

I want you to breathe a sigh of relief.

Remember, this ministry journey is a long one. We want to make sure we finish our race well—not just rush through every *"check-point"* as fast as possible.

Growing in relationship with a leader is a vulnerable process. It shouldn't be rushed for influence or clout.

It's not about a famous name, green room access, or social media following.

It's about finding someone whose life you feel like you can truly follow.

That person might not have a *"huge"* church or a million dollars in the bank, but they are sincere and kind.

They treat people with respect.

And they have a heart to serve everyone around them—even those who are supposed to be serving them.

This may even end up being a friend that's your own age.

Remember, it's about finding a voice in your life that you trust.

They might not always be the obvious choice for *"loyalty nominations,"* but they have fruit that remains in their life.

When it comes down to it, I think that's one of the best ways to steward the purity of our loyalty: **are we people who honor the tree that the fruit comes from... or do we just honor the fruit?**

The difference here is loyalty that's rooted, **versus loyalty that's**

seasonal.

Loyalty that's rooted means we see the fruit in someone's life and understand it comes from somewhere deep inside them.

Those deep roots are where the amazing facets of that person are really hidden. The fruit is wonderful, but it's really just external proof of what's going on inside—what's not always obvious or public.

The seasonal form of loyalty?

It's about grabbing all the fruit we can, **just to use it.**

We learn how someone speaks, only so we can become better speakers. Or we find a minister with a large following and mimic their methods, just to get a large following too.

Whether or not they're a good person off the stage doesn't really affect us, because we just want the results.

So we try to use our loyalty as a ladder— If we rub the right shoulders long enough, the higher we'll go.

Another facet of seasonal loyalty is this:
When the fruit disappears, so does the loyalty.

We find another tree down the street, or in another city, that's in its *"harvest season,"* and go after their fruit next.

Even though many of us would agree this isn't the road we should take, many of us fall into its trap more than we realize.

But if we make a conscious effort to celebrate the human—not just the pastoral title—or the amazing heart—not just the worship-leading gift—then we'll **not only have healthier loyalty to leaders but to the people around us in general.**

Now, as much as I love the story of the red chair, I also have no problem admitting the danger of becoming so loyal that it blurs your perspective and decision-making.

Remember when we talked about mislabeling enemies?
How you can give a spiritual enemy a human face?

Well, I equally believe we can give Jesus a leader's face.

We can downgrade the cornerstone of our souls into the human form of our pastors, heroes, and beyond.

If we're not careful, when they speak, **we can assume it's the same as Jesus saying it.**

But it doesn't matter who our leader is—they're not batting a thousand.

Their boss might be God, but they're not twins.

Have you ever heard the old adage, *"A broken clock is right at least twice a day"*?

That's how I think we should feel about leaders in ministry.

Even the *"worst"* ones can still hit a home run now and then.

And we shouldn't confuse those successes as stamps of approval from God on their actions or philosophies.

The Bible is full of stories where God used people for amazing things... But most of their character traits and backstories leave us scratching our heads.

Our leaders aren't always that different from those puzzling examples.

Someone being used by God doesn't mean they're the perfect example to follow in all areas of life.

So, how do we set ourselves up for a healthy balance between these varying levels of loyalty and who we give it to?

I'd like to start by highlighting two facets of the red chair concept that are important to keep in mind:

1.) If you're serving a healthy leader, they'll usually let you know if you're becoming too loyal. They'd **probably try to stop you from even buying the red paint in the first place.** Often, they've already made their own *"black chair"* statement — inviting you to consider a bigger picture beyond that moment. One you can only discover through ongoing relationship and honest questions.

2.) Then there are *"less healthy"* leaders who'd love nothing more than for people to let their ideas run unchecked. Their **imagination runs wild with all the possibilities that kind of loyalty brings *(scary, but true)*.**

"Dear friends, do not believe every spirit, but test the spirits to see whether they are from God, because many false prophets have gone out into the world." (1 John 4:1)

If you read that and feel worried because you're not sure where your leaders fit, here's some good news: **awareness is half the battle.**

Think about walking across train tracks without knowing the schedule or wearing headphones so you can't hear the train coming.

It's not the tracks that put you in danger — **it's the lack of awareness.**

Ministry often works the same way.

1 Peter 5:8 says, *"Be alert and of sober mind. Your enemy the devil prowls around like a roaring lion looking for someone to devour."*

What are we supposed to be alert toward?

That the enemy is on a mission — not just existing — but actively hunting.

So here's a tool: **awareness can keep you safe.**

If our hearts recognize the possibility of being manipulated or taken advantage of, we're already in a safer place to serve our leaders.

From there, we're free to be loyal — **but without ignorance.**

We can cheer for them without blindly signing off on everything they believe or do.

Maybe someone has incredible theological insight, but you don't agree with how they handle their marriage or family. Or maybe they're a powerful speaker, but you've seen them struggle as a pastor of people.

What do we do?

We do something called, *"chew the meat and spit out the bones."*

It means taking time to separate what's good for us to digest from what might be harmful.

We practice this in sermons, staff meetings, books, and countless other places. We learn from their strengths while guarding our hearts from their flaws.

There's a difference between being loyal from a heart of service and thinking loyalty proves how pure our service is.

One keeps perspective anchored.
The other thinks perspective gets in the way or slows you down.

I've personally seen how the *"chew the meat"* method saves us from a lot of unnecessary turmoil.

We don't lose the joy of serving people because a leader has flaws.

Instead, we serve with a more stable joy — **rooted in the perfect leadership of Jesus.**

Colossians 3:17 says, *"And whatever you do, whether in word or deed, do it all in the name of the Lord Jesus, giving thanks to God the Father through him."*

When we remember His perfection, we don't need other leaders to fill His shoes.

There's an interesting tug-of-war when you trust God with where He has you in your ministry journey.

Sometimes you work with people you feel you'll be close to for the rest of your lives. Other times, you're not sure you'll make it through the next Easter production without an emotional breakdown.

In this journey, it's not just about where you are, **but who you're around — and why.**

I've grown so much from leaders whose personalities and decision-making skills I'd hope to never operate in myself.

But honoring their roots — without tripping over the rotten apples — **is key to becoming healthier myself.**

The leaders we serve week-in and week-out can be pillars in our ministry story — if we allow them to be. As long as we don't let those pillars turn into giant statues of robotic agreement or stubborn resentment.

Let them be what they are: **a part of the story.**

Not the story.
Just a part.

No one should throw away a whole book because one page didn't meet expectations.

So go ahead—paint all the chairs you want!

Find amazing people and celebrate what you love about them.

Ask questions and chew on their answers.

Enjoy being someone who doesn't feel like they need to know

everything.

Honor well. Honor smart.

Let your leaders expand the boundaries of what you see in life and ministry.

Who knows... **all those chairs might even look better in red.**

CHAPTER SEVEN

PASSIVE AGGRESSIVE 101

———

emotional shepherding

"Crazy" rubs off.

Not like you can scrub it away with effort, but if you're around some unsavory behavior long enough, it slowly becomes your own.

It sneaks in.
It can actually rub off on you.

Don't believe me?

Ever met someone who complains about everything? They don't agree with anyone's choices and feel like the world's against them.

Then, six months later, they're friends with someone who starts sounding just like that—talking and feeling the same way.

How does that happen?

Maybe they share the same personality type, sure.
But more often, one gets influenced by the other.

The personality they picked up becomes the identity they live by.

"Walk with the wise and become wise, for a companion of fools suffers harm." (Proverbs 13:20)

That's a heavy truth.

I first learned this lesson when I started traveling and leading worship.

Picture a bus full of college students, all of us figuring it out as we went. Several weekends away from home and class, seeing God move through different churches.

You can imagine how crammed youthful personalities and the emotional weight of ministering multiple times in a row created plenty of *"drama."*

Honestly? I loved watching it all unfold.

It was hilarious.

Things like *"who got to sing a solo"* turned into full-blown debates.

Common sense and logic left the room, replaced by competitive biographies of who was the most *"Christ-like"* when they sang.

I just sat back, eating my imaginary popcorn, watching people stake their self-worth on a forty-five-second solo.

How could you not find that entertaining?

But no matter the drama's topic, I noticed something strange: even without yelling or outright insults, some odd little remarks would surface.

Not spoken like speeches, but whispered enough to make sure you caught the meaning—just quiet enough not to sound arrogant.

Lines like:
- *"That's an odd choice for a soloist, but whatever."*
- *"Wow, they must be really passionate about that song."*
- *"I don't even care that much, but apparently it's their whole world."*

Those phrases left me tilting my head, wondering, What did they mean by that?

I call this **"Passive Aggressive 101"**— the subtle, cowardly way **people vent frustration without owning it.**

What frustrations?

That's the million-dollar question.

Often, it's impossible to pinpoint what's behind those words—who they're aimed at, why, or when. Sometimes, the frustration isn't even about you, yet you get caught in the crossfire.

And here's the kicker: **sometimes, you're the one tossing others into your own frustration's path.**

Think of your emotional capacity like a cup.

You can only pour so much in before it spills over.

A passive-aggressive spill-over happens when we don't face or understand our inner emotional dialogue.

It sneaks out in little snips of negativity—snapping at someone for not answering an email when really, we're upset about a comment they made weeks ago.

How do we miss our own overflow?

We're distracted.
Especially by busy-ness.

If ministry teaches you anything, **it's how to stay busy.**

No matter how much you do, there's always more that could be done.

Visit a hundred people in the hospital, and your brain latches onto the one you didn't see. Then you go home, trying to enjoy a quiet evening with family, but your mind hasn't unplugged yet.

You catch yourself thinking, *"I hope they know I wanted to visit today if I hadn't been so busy."* Or worse, *"Maybe I should go see them now and relax later."*

Here's the truth: there is always more to do.

There will always be someone else to help, more time to give, more sacrifice to make.

So, feeling busy isn't just about the work on your plate—it's about the work still out there, waiting.

The sheer volume can make you want to nap just thinking about it.

But you don't.
You push through.

You remind yourself why you do this.
You sip your coffee in between.

But here's where we get caught: busy-ness distracts us from how our emotions handle the weight of these *"holy responsibilities."*

I saw this firsthand in a meeting with a *"ministry veteran."*

They'd been running full-force for decades, leaving behind an amazing legacy.

One day, we sat down to plan some upcoming events, but when they arrived, I noticed they looked completely worn out.

Maybe it was a long trip, or something like that.
Whatever it was, it was obvious.

So, my southern manners kicked in: *"Are you doing alright? You look pretty tired."*

They finished a quick text, let out an exhale chuckle, and said, *"I live tired."*

I wasn't sure how to respond, so I awkwardly laughed and said something like, *"I know that's right!"*

But I was thrown off.

Remember the Bible verse, *"Come to me, all you who are weary and burdened, and I will give you rest." (Matthew 11:28-30)* ?

Well, they seemed way more *"weary"* than *"rested."*

They knew they were tired. **But they didn't seem bothered enough to change it.**

And that bothered me.

Not because I have a problem with a can-do attitude *(quite the opposite)*.

But because it was clear there was a rhythm in place—a pattern—that let them ignore how their body and mind were handling the load.

Their focus on positive outcomes distracted them from how they were getting there.

If we're not careful, busy and tired become badges of honor—not to brag, but to prove we're *"good and faithful servants."*

Don't get me wrong: work is part of life, ministry or not.

But maybe it's worth asking ourselves, every now and then: **Am I tired because I'm tired... or am I tired because I don't know a better way to do this?**

Sometimes, not having an answer can be the biggest distraction of all.

If we distract ourselves through busy-ness, and our emotional cup is starting to reach its limit, where can we find the first hint of passive-aggressive danger?

I'd say it's in blaming others.

Harsh start, I know.

And I'm not talking about plotting someone's downfall.

It's more about giving our emotions a chance to exhale—in a *"controlled environment."*

It's never in statements that are overtly obvious.
The poison is always beneath the surface.

Passive aggression is dull words with sharp edges—an undertone that communicates more than the actual words do.

It starts in our imagination with phrases like, *"I can't believe I have to work so hard, when they barely do anything."* or *"They only got a promotion because they kiss up to leadership."*

But it comes out in words like, *"You look like you're enjoying yourself."* or *"I guess you're Mr. Popular, huh?"*

The words seem subtle—but the punch they pack usually isn't.

When we're on the receiving end of comments like these, we might think, *"Those people must be pretty insecure to say something like that."*

But if someone calls us out for the same thing?

We think, *"Why are they being so sensitive?"*

We tend to put the problem outside ourselves, never inside.

Have you ever considered the life of a shepherd?

It's monotonous. Demanding.

Requires so much attention and care.

They spend every day looking after sheep—responsible for animals that get trapped easily, wander off, or get attacked.

But imagine that the shepherd is you, and the sheep are your emotions — can you see any similarities in how they might operate:
- How easily your emotions can get stuck in a cycle of thinking.
- How one emotion can run off, leaving the others behind.
- And that's all before something comes to attack your emotions.

If one shepherd blamed another for the state of their flock, we'd see how flawed that is.

They should take responsibility for their own sheep.

Other shepherds have their own flocks to care for.
They can't pause their work to fix ours.

Getting the picture?

When we choose to shepherd our emotions consciously, we're one step closer to managing the water in our cup.

We notice when feelings of *"lack of recognition"* try to jump over the fence.

We pause to bring them back into the flock. And since we're watching our fatigue, we can see how the whole flock of emotions is doing—together.

BAIT TRAPS

But what if you're doing the hard work of shepherding—and the problem is the shepherd across the street?

Your flocks once coexisted in peace, but now there's friction.

They make statements that attack your flock of emotions, tricking you into leaving yours behind so you can cross over and retaliate.

They say things, not because they believe them, but because they know it'll stir a reaction.

Your reaction becomes their reward.

This is where I remind myself—*"Don't take the bait."*

People passionate about fishing are passionate about bait—not because bait is interesting—but because they know the exact match between bait and fish.

Want a specific result?
You need a specific method.

Some people use passive-aggressive tactics the same way.

They mix words and timing just right to lure your emotions—**until you're hooked.**

You say things you shouldn't.
And all because *"But they said…"*

Ephesians 4:15 says it well: *"Instead, speaking the truth in love, we will grow to become in every respect the mature body of him who is the head, that is, Christ."*

No one truly wins these verbal battles.
Everyone ends up looking immature, fragile.

And because we're all busy, there's no time to dig into the real issues.

So if we enter conversations passive-aggressively, we probably leave the same way—**pouring more water into an already overflowing cup.**

Just imagine how that grows over time.

I want to pause here and remind us: **We're cultivating a mindset for longevity in ministry.**

That means approaching reality—not the forever kind, but the reality that might be the most likely to initially happen.

Co-workers aren't evil or out to get you.

But people *(including you and me)* have human traits that sometimes get in the way.

Here, we're learning healthier ways to navigate those hurdles—**not just pointing them out.**

If someone has a bad day and asks for prayer, we naturally give grace. But what if that bad day stretches into a whole year? Our grace might start to run thin.

And what if they never ask for prayer because they're embarrassed? We don't know why they're moody.

Would we still give grace, or wait to be asked? Or at least need some context to understand why patience is necessary?
These are the real questions we're tackling.

When we talk about passive aggression, it might sound like *"Some people are crazy, here's how to avoid them."*

But that's not it.

People do crazy things.
There's almost always a why behind it.

So let's not let their crazy today ruin our relationship tomorrow. And vice versa.

We have a cup that needs emptying—**regularly.**

Maybe that means creating space for honest feedback with a leader. Or making sure when we get home, we're fully present with our family—knowing only Jesus meets every need, all the time.

We also have emotions that need shepherding.

It's not enough that they're all together on your field—we have to actively care for their well-being.

Maybe it's stepping away from a conversation to splash cold water on our face and breathe. Or sneaking off to our car to listen to worship and let our soul catch its breath before our words do their work.

I once heard a pastor say, *"I've had leaders that gave grace to my humanity, so when they let their humanity show, I want to repay the favor."*

Wow. That says it all.

Colossians 3:13 reminds us: *"Bear with each other and forgive one another if any of you has a grievance against someone. Forgive as the Lord forgave you."*

Passive aggression is a bottomless pit.
It grows as long as anyone feeds it.

But if we refuse to take the bait—and choose grace for ourselves and others—**I have a feeling grace will grow right in its place.**

CHAPTER EIGHT

LET PEOPLE FAIL

---

growing fruit

In case you couldn't tell by the title of this chapter, what follows might be some of the hardest content for you to digest in this entire book.

A good opportunity to test out your new ability to *"chew the meat and spit out the bones,"* in case you need it.

I'm a huge believer in letting people fail.

I mean royally.

I mean in ways they will never forget for the rest of their lives.

Now, before you assume something different than what I'm actually saying, I want to be clear: **I'm definitely not talking about failing morally or in a way that damages yourself or others.**

When it comes to *"failing in ministry,"* our minds can automatically go there. But that's not the kind of failing I mean.

I'm talking about failure that produces growth—**both individually and corporately.**

I remember when I was first learning how to swim.

I grew up in a time that was, let's just say, a little less concerned about *"feelings"* than we are today.

If you want to understand how different, my swim story will help paint the picture.

Like most things I wanted to do, I first saw them on TV or in movies.

If someone I thought was cool was riding a bike, I wanted to ride one too. If I saw a superhero flying, my response was to grab an umbrella, climb on the roof, and see if I could float down. Just a baby step toward my own flight technique.

(This is actually a true story, and yes, it involved a beach umbrella—which I thought would create a parachute effect. Spoiler: it didn't.)

So, when I saw some Mark Twain characters swimming in a river, naturally, I decided I wanted to try. It didn't look too complicated, and I had the gusto to see it through.

My dad and older brother said they'd teach me, and even they didn't think it would take me long to get the hang of it.

All that was left was to find a good hotel pool we could crash.

I'll never forget putting on bulky floaties that left my arms suspended in mid-air, goggles way too tight, and an obscene amount of sunscreen.

But even with all that, I could tell—**this was my moment.**

I couldn't wait to hear the applause as I swam at least a hundred laps. They asked if I was ready, and I let out a resounding, *"Yes!"*

I thought we'd all get in together, then they'd break down the mechanics before watching me soar. Unfortunately, before I knew it, I had been picked up and thrown into the deep end.

By myself.

Yes, you read that right.

They didn't jump in with me—I was thrown in solo.

Think Daniel in the lion's den, **but with a kid screaming.**

A few seconds later, I felt them jump in and lift my head above the water.

I had failed—and apparently, they found it extremely entertaining.

They gave me a quick pep talk and told me they'd do it again. I immediately started begging for mercy.

I couldn't help but be angry at myself for such an idiotic idea. Umbrella parachuting was safer than this.

But my family wasn't one for letting excuses keep you from doing something. So through tears, they tossed me again—**only this time, my panic was cut in half.**

They arrived a few seconds later, just like before. And I started to feel something rising inside me.

It wasn't confidence in myself, exactly, but a growing trust that my dad and brother would make sure I didn't drown.

Before long, they were still throwing me in, but my tears slowly turned to laughter.

What had started as a nightmare became a free fall into **trying something without the fear that failure meant death.**

I wasn't a natural swimmer, but I did swim.

It wasn't pretty. It wasn't something that could save someone else from drowning. But it was enough—**enough to give me the confidence to try again.**

This is how I want us to think about letting people fail.

For people to grow into who they believe they can be, they need an environment where failure doesn't equal elimination.

Trying something and failing doesn't mean you get fired or demoted—in reality <u>or in relationship.</u>

But this requires insight on both sides—**those attempting the risk outside their comfort zone, and those allowing the attempt.**

Ministry can be full of stressful environments and high demands.

A desire for excellence can easily slip into a bondage of paranoia.

Before you know it, we're consumed with thoughts and conversations that sound purely motivated—but have been mixed with something else.

Something that puts more responsibility in our hands than in God's hands.

I've frankly always believed that what many call *"excellence,"* I could translate as just... *"expensive."*

The more money we spend on a production or event, the more ministers comment on its *"excellence factors."* But I've seen churches with a five-dollar budget and pure-hearted volunteers exude excellence over and over again.

Regardless of resources, there's a voice inside our heads whispering, *"This needs to go perfectly."*

It comes from the nervous idea that we're always being watched.

And those watching need to see something perfect—usually because we believe eternity depends on it.

The Bible draws powerful parallels between how we live and how people view God: *"By this everyone will know that you are my disciples, if you love one another." (John 13:35)* and *"Let your light shine before others, that they may see your good deeds and glorify your Father in heaven." (Matthew 5:16)*

This truth is powerful because it empowers us to give people who've never heard about Jesus a small window into His generous compassion and love—by showing it through our daily behavior and character.

But sometimes, we let it evolve beyond its intention.

We begin to think that if a light bulb goes out on our stage during service, or a microphone battery dies mid-sermon, **we've dropped the excellence ball.**

Instead of seeing a mishap as a simple mistake, we worry people will see it as proof that we don't care about doing things properly.

Which then communicates that God must not care about doing things properly either.

Do you see how quickly this snowballs?

When we slip into this version of excellence, it's rooted in the idea that we make God proud by how we perform.

We've heard scriptures like, *"While we were still sinners, Christ died for us." (Romans 5:8)* and *"For by grace you have been saved through faith... not of works, lest anyone should boast." (Ephesians 2:8-9)*

But still, we think if we sing pretty enough, build our small group big enough, or get more people saved next week than last, God will add a gold star to His love for us.

This mindset is the biggest barrier to giving people—and ourselves—the space to fail.

We don't believe we have any *"fail space"* to spare.

God deserves our best, and we're not going to waste time on someone we're unsure can execute their gift at a high level.

Sounds fair, doesn't it?
But what does this promote?

I remember once working with a large church that held extremely high standards for excellence. They firmly believed that someone who had never been to their church before needed to have a seamless experience—from start to finish.

So, a service wasn't just meticulously planned the week before; it was also dissected the following Monday morning.

What went perfectly was acknowledged, and what didn't... **got dissected.**

They would say things like, *"**The parking lot has got to be clear before people arrive for the second service, or they will never come back because they couldn't park fast enough.**"*

Now, obviously no one wants to spend twenty minutes stuck in a parking lot, so there was validity to the concern. But sometimes, it felt like **we were becoming paranoid about the idea of a problem more than an actual problem.**

Everything had a *"holy angle"* for why we needed to critique it so thoroughly, but it didn't take long for me to notice that this often sucked the joy right out of ministry.

It made working for God <u>feel a lot more like work.</u>

Then before you knew it, we were just clocking in and clocking out—getting through one more service just in time to plan the next one.

We paid more attention to the way a band sounded than to the people singing the songs in the congregation.

Not exactly the most life-giving rhythm.

In a church this size, there would always be someone who wanted to serve.

Getting their info was easy.
Getting them involved?

That was harder.

And the closer their involvement had anything to do with the stage, the harder it became.

We had a standard, and that standard could not be compromised. So it didn't matter how pure your heart was. What mattered was the strength of your ability—**particularly a strength you'd already built before you arrived.**

That was usually the perfect option for us.

Someone who could give, **but not someone who would need.**

Anyone outside that definition fell between the cracks.

Now, I want to say there was a lot in their thought process I fully understood—and even agreed with sometimes. There were several other churches I'd been with that echoed similar sentiments.

We didn't want to take advantage of someone's willingness to serve by putting them in a situation they weren't ready for.

That is not the type of failure that leads to growth. That's just plain cruelty.

But if you put someone in a scenario they don't know if they can handle—but you believe they can—that will almost always lead to positive experiences that make them less afraid next time.

And if you're not sure what they can handle, letting them grow gradually in *"less risky"* environments is usually wise.

For example: if someone wants to sing a solo and they have a good voice, you need to know how their nerves affect their ability.

So you wouldn't give them *"O Holy Night"* in front of a thousand people to see how they respond. You'd let them sing a solo during the worship portion of a kids' service instead.

Because if you can survive singing to a bunch of kids, **you can usually survive anything.**

THOUGHTFUL THINKING

There is a real fear of failure.

Not just a public failure, but one we believe reflects a perfect God.

So it makes sense why we're not eager to allow some *"less-perfect"* moments in a ministry service.

But how do we allow real space—and still uphold a standard?

I suggest we become consistent in intentionality.

When I was in my early twenties, I was put in charge of a worship team filled with talent and potential.

But I quickly noticed that when they had a chance to step out and take charge of their song or moment, they cowarded.

Through conversations, I found out the previous leader had requested all major leading moments on stage happen through them alone.

So, even though team members felt they could do something amazing with their song when they led it, they were used to a rhythm of thought that said only one person gets to shine on stage—**and it wasn't them.**

In all honesty, when I hear that kind of mindset, I tend to push for a dramatic shift in the opposite direction.

Some things require patience.
Others demand action.

To me, this was action all the way.

I started using a catchphrase to push their thinking: *"I'm not going to save you."*

If they wanted to step into their potential, they had to do it with confidence.

If they wanted to pray at the end of the song, give encouragement, or spontaneously start singing the chorus of a different song—great.

But if they realized it was a mistake and couldn't get out of it in that moment, they had to sit in the awkwardness... or learn to pivot.

All while looking at the faces of the congregation, staring back in curiosity or confusion.

I know many reading this might think it sounds like a cruel experiment.

But hear my heart: If someone wants to take a risk, they need to understand **every risk isn't a success.**

Sometimes it goes great.
Sometimes it doesn't.

That's not bad.
It's just life.

In ministry or out, it rings true.

If you never feel the sting of a failed risk, I believe you lose respect for the people you're risking in front of.

If you know a leader will step in and sing the chorus everyone likes to save you from a confused room listening to a chorus no one has heard before—**you have no reason to think twice before singing it in the first place.**

Then what you get is someone elevating an idea over the person the idea is supposed to be for.

That doesn't grow anyone.

People who minister have to be thinkers.

Not just about what they want to do or what feels best to try, but about the people they're doing it in front of—**and if it's helpful to them.**

This team had been robbed of their ability to think **because they knew they never needed to.**

The previous leader did all the risking and stole their growth simultaneously.

So they had to learn how to think, so they could learn how to risk.

Before long, this sparked tons of behind-the-scenes conversations and questions that opened the team's eyes to possibilities they hadn't realized before.

It took time.
I didn't mind that at all.

In fairness, a lot of it fits my personality—I can stare at an awkward moment on stage and not flinch.

But even if you can't relate to that feeling, the fruit that followed should be evidence enough: **People were growing.**

Not because they came that way automatically, but because they had space to become who they could be if given the opportunity.

They felt safe.

They felt a confidence that failure wouldn't *"kill them."*

I think two things are monumentally important:
1) Busyness does not automatically equal productivity.
2) Results are not the same as fruit.

When we're doing a lot, we think that means we're doing a lot.

We're running full force, letting our sweat shine with pride.

But what if we recognized we've only been running on a treadmill? Running hard but gaining no ground.

In the same way, someone may be performing but not growing. And this is where we have an amazing opportunity.

The growth of the people around us is one of the most fulfilling parts of ministry **I've ever experienced.**

The only thing that can make it better is when the person doesn't see in themselves what you see.

It's like seeing a preview of a movie before it comes out.

You don't know every detail, but you have an idea—**and that's enough to get you excited about what's coming.**

We have a pretty good idea of what happens when we remain paranoid about perfection.

We see examples everywhere.

We have fewer examples of people who are growing wide AND deep, but those examples are worth the space to let them flourish.

Who knew that sometimes **the best fertilizer is failure?**

CHAPTER NINE

RAISE YOUR PRO-DUCTION VALUE

---

honor the human

What comes to mind when you hear the phrase *"raise your production value"*?

More often than not, we assume it means ramping up the lights, cameras, and all the razzle-dazzle.

But what if I told you it could mean something else?

What if raising production value is actually about highlighting the individuals and teams who make all those things happen?

We're really talking about **raising the value we have for the people** behind the production angles of ministry.

In two decades of ministry, I've seen plenty of personalities, crowd sizes, budgets, and levels of notoriety.

But one thing stands out across the board: **Production staff and volunteers — especially sound engineers — are often treated terribly.**

It doesn't happen everywhere, and I've seen many exceptions. But if there's one thing I've witnessed with the most consistency, it's this.

Now, before you dismiss this idea, thinking, *"My ministry doesn't really do a lot of fireworks and smoke, so this probably doesn't apply to me"*, hear me out.

Even if you livestream from your phone in your living room, or use a microphone plugged into a karaoke machine in the middle of the jungle... All of that falls under what I call the *"production umbrella."*

There's technique behind it.

Sometimes it requires personnel to run or assist.

And how we treat those people? That's a big deal.

A big deal that needs a fresh look.

Where does the disconnect come from when it comes to production teams and how they're treated?

I'm sure there are many reasons, but a couple stand out to me right away.

First, people in production tend to be behind-the-scenes types. They're fascinated by technology — wires, software, the science underneath it all.

They almost never want the spotlight.

They just want to work on the things they love.

Building and watching those things evolve forward—**that's their reward.**

But if you're someone used to the stage and the spotlight, these quiet, tech-loving personalities can seem... odd.

Their quietness might be mistaken for disinterest.
Their dry humor might come off as arrogance.

Here's another layer: production teams usually take pride in their craft. They want things done right — **done well.**

But in ministry, sometimes people want things done the easy way.

Fast and cheap decisions?

Nails on a chalkboard for someone who believes in doing it with integrity.

And then, production teams get asked to perform miracles with these *"fast and cheap"* options—to suddenly make it look expensive and planned.

I've lost count of how many times I've heard leaders say, *"This is what we have and this is what I want—figure it out."*

What's wild is that production teams actually pull these miracles off.

Time after time.

Because they're that skilled and determined.

But that only **feeds into a broken mindset** in leadership around production process.

Unfortunately, those long hours and that intelligence don't always get the respect and acknowledgment they deserve.

Far too often, these people and their sacrifices are neglected — even, if I'm honest, **abused.**

I want to share a story that stuck with me.

A pastor — let's call him Shawn — told me about a sound engineer named Brett.

When Brett started at Shawn's church, Shawn quickly learned Brett had been mistreated by several other churches before.

Shawn made it his mission to mend Brett's confidence and wounds.

He made sure Brett was treated with dignity by the staff and celebrated for his hard work.

Over the years, **Brett grew and blossomed.**

Then came a job opportunity at another church, with better pay and a chance to develop his skills.

Shawn and Brett both felt it was time to turn the page.

They parted as friends, blessing each other's next chapters.

A beautiful story, right?

But a few months later, Shawn started getting texts and calls from Brett.

The mistreatment he'd escaped was happening again.

The depression was settling in.
Brett was nearing his breaking point.

Shawn tried to help — offering counsel, scripture, encouragement. He pleaded with Brett to quit, find another job, or even a new career. But Brett said he could handle it. **Maybe he was just overthinking it.**

Months went by.

Then Shawn heard the news: Brett had committed suicide.

Shawn was paralyzed with grief and haunted by questions — *"What could I have done?"*

Anger burned toward the leaders who had emotionally and verbally abused Brett. But Shawn realized it wasn't that simple.

Those leaders weren't the whole story, but their words and actions brought more harm when they could have brought healing.

Later, while preaching at a church conference, Shawn shared Brett's story through tears.

He begged ministers to choose kindness when speaking to their production teams.

Because we never really know what someone is dealing with.

Our words can heal... or hurt.

For better or for worse.

This story has stayed in my heart ever since I first heard it.

Honestly, it was the main reason I wanted to write this chapter.

I'm not here to stir up a debate about mental illness or who's to blame. But I do want us to pause and ask ourselves: **How do we see the people who work on production?**

These are the folks running our song lyrics, checking microphone batteries, building props for Easter musicals—and everything in between.

They're brilliant people with huge hearts.

But how do we talk to them?
How do we really see them?

Are they skilled craftsmen... or just the ones who turn the volume up?

Do they create graphics that elevate our sermons... or do they just mess around on their computers all day, and we wonder why we even pay them?

Of course, no one's flawless.

They might have bad days, miss the pastor's vision, or go down a YouTube rabbit hole sometimes.

But do we see the human behind it all?

Their feelings, dreams, and passion?

Or do they get lost behind what they do?

I've always found it fascinating how parts of the Bible show how the mindset of a time period or culture can blur the full impact of a miracle.

My mind goes straight to Jesus and the loaves and fishes.

When this story's preached, you'll often hear that it wasn't just five thousand people fed.

Why?

Because back then, women and children weren't counted the same way in crowds. So when God fed five thousand, it might have been twenty thousand or more.

That difference? Huge.

If you've ever been to a concert with five thousand people—and then one with twenty thousand—you know exactly how much bigger that feels.

This is the power of our thinking.

Not just in realizing who is impacted, but in remembering **who was always part of the story.**

Those women and children? Always there.

But someone decided they didn't matter enough to make the headlines.

I'm worried we can fall into a similar trap.

We think there are those who serve in ministry... and those who __do__ ministry.

Notice that difference?

We see a preacher on stage and say, *"Now that's ministry."*

But what about the person who set up the sound system so the preacher's voice could be heard?

Is that ministry?
Or just serving a ministry?

I get it—answers differ depending on the situation.

Sometimes ministries hire *"outside talent"* who might not even be believers. So it's hard to think of them as *"fellow ministers,"* especially compared to a seminary grad preaching on stage.

But I want to invite us all to consider this: **Are we cutting people out of the story?**

God is doing miracles every week—salvations and more—but sometimes we leave people out by how we edit the story. Because we think their part isn't that important.

There's freedom here, if you look at Matthew 4:18-22.

Jesus walks by the Sea of Galilee, sees Simon (Peter) and Andrew fishing, and says, *"Follow me, and I will make you fishers of men."*

Jesus tells fishermen they'll keep fishing...

but now for something different.

The skill stays the same.

But now there's a revelation: their work has Kingdom purpose.

Suddenly, something that doesn't look spiritual becomes deeply spiritual.

Imagine telling someone trained to build stages for arenas, *"You're not just building stages for concerts—you can build stages for God. Same skills. But now for God."*

Their passion doesn't have to be left at the altar of ministry.
It can be their ministry.

They don't have to quit running lights for popular bands to serve a small church just to prove their heart for God.

How they treat their team and the bands can be a form of evangelism.

Their work hasn't changed—only their belief that Jesus empowers them through it.

And we can be the voices that remind them of that.

Not voices demanding perfection or obedience, but voices of empowerment for people with so much to give.

DREAM TOGETHER

Now, before you get too excited and start pushing your production team to dream big—know this: **They'll likely have no problem reaching as high as you'll let them.**

But that means sometimes they'll dream beyond budgets, talent, and resources.

That's okay.
You still invite them to dream.

But the best dreaming happens with communication.

Say something like, *"For Christmas this year, I want to try something different. In a dream scenario, what would you do?"*

Give them a few minutes to shoot for the stars.

Take notes.

Then ask, *"Okay, if you could pick only two ideas from that, what would they be?"*

Let them think.

Listen.

Finally, ask, *"How can we make those happen with what we have—budget, people, resources?"*

Sure, it won't be their perfect dream.
It might even feel pointless at first.

But this is where creativity stretches its muscles.

This is where they see you care about their ideas—and their expertise.

Suddenly, they're not minions. **They're ministers.**

Can you imagine if someone had insulted the boy who gave his lunch to feed over twenty thousand people?

Can you imagine how Jesus would have responded?

For someone to give what little they had... and then someone complains about waiting in line for their free meal?

Not a good look.

But think about it: **this boy fed a crowd that didn't even think he deserved to be counted.**

A miracle happened through his willingness—**and the people impacted forgot to include him in their gratitude.**

That's not where we want to be.

We want to be the first to express heartfelt appreciation and inspiration to the one who puts what's in their hands into Jesus' hands. Because that usually means **we're about to be impacted by it**—in all its glorious forms.

Ministry can be stressful.

And where stress runs high, words get loose.

Attitudes run unchecked.
Requests turn into demands.

The first to feel that weight? **Often the production team.**

If we have the power to protect them, let's do it—as much as possible.

Yes, the work still needs to get done.
It always will.

But the way we go about it is always up for debate.

Let's be on the right side.

Our messages are published on podcasts.
Our songs are recorded.
Our sanctuaries are lit.

And the Gospel expands through it all.

All thanks to a group of people waiting for Jesus to pass by their boat... **to give them permission to fish in a completely new way.**

So let's raise our production value—who they are and what they do.

Jesus just might use it to feed the crowds.

CHAPTER TEN

FIGHTING GHOSTS

when people leave

Have you ever tried to **punch the air?**

Trying to take out your anger on things you can't physically grasp?

Letting out your aggression but not actually hitting anything?

It sounds kind of funny when you think about it.

Picture this: you're walking down the sidewalk, minding your own business, and suddenly you spot someone **throwing right hooks into nothing.**

Every swing comes with a grunt and heavy breathing as they reset for the next round.

I think it's safe to say most of us would discreetly slide over to the other side of the street.

Paul says in 1 Corinthians 9:26-27, *"I do not run aimlessly; I do not box as one beating the air. But I discipline my body and keep it under control, lest after preaching to others I myself should be disqualified."*

In this passage, Paul points out the difference between understanding something in theory and actually living it out.

It's possible to get the concept but forget to let it sink deep into your daily life. And that's how you end up with a soul exhausted from all the air punching.

I can't help but see a parallel here with what happens when people leave the ministries we serve.

When a team is working together, we pour our energy into the people physically present — building them up, growing relationships. But often, we're haunted by the *"ghosts"* of amazing people who are no longer there.

And that struggle—whether it's wrestling with painful memories **or idolizing the good ones**—can make us feel aimless.

Like we can't move forward from where we are.

People leave for many reasons, but I want to focus on three main categories: Death, Failure, or Growth.

The first category is arguably the most complicated, so I'll spend the most time there.

Life keeps moving, and then suddenly, a leader, friend, mentor, or confidant passes away. Grief crashes in alongside questions like, *"What now?"* and *"Where do we go from here?"*

I've only experienced one major event like this in my ministry so far. But it hit me hard enough to drive the point home.

I was in college—right at the epicenter of emotional confusion and aimless vision.

The future freaked me out.

There were only a few places where I could catch my breath above the clouds of uncertainty and doubt about the perfect will of God for my life.

One of those places was the campus ministry choir, led by a man we mentioned earlier—Dr. David Horton.

Dr. Horton was a genius—naive, friendly, grouchy, heartfelt, insensitive—**all at the same time.**

That mix made him magnetic—someone you overlooked the challenges with, because the whole package was fascinating.

College feels like the first time you get permission to look beyond your familiar world for answers. I have amazing parents who give great advice, but Dr. Horton was the first person outside my family I truly opened up to.

We had just a few conversations (*he could be intimidating*), but they stuck with me, like moments I'd never forget.

One afternoon, I was at my wit's end.

I left class in the middle of a lecture and rushed to his office. I unloaded my usual struggle: too many interests, no clue which path was right.

He gave me some sage advice. Then, as I got up to leave, I reached out to shake his hand—*(blame my southern manners)*.

He shook it, looked me straight in the eye, and said, *"Trust Him. It's not your job to worry about it."*

My brain instantly started chewing on that.

I thought, *"Yeah, I know that… duh!"* and *"Wow, that's so true!"* all at once.

Then, unexpectedly, he pulled me in for a hug.

I was honestly shocked.

Dr. Horton wasn't known for being the hugging type, but this felt intentional, maybe even led by God.

I took it anyway and, for a week, felt borderline famous for it.

A couple months later, Dr. Horton passed away—shockingly— while leading a ministry trip in the Bahamas.

I had just finished my sophomore year, and my mentor—the guy who was supposed to guide me—**was gone.**

Not just from my life, but from leading the ministry I loved.

It felt like being on a boat with no sails, no engine, no compass.

Over the next months, the school tried to fill his role for the next semester.

The new leaders were great people, with sincere hearts. But students had trusted Dr. Horton's vision deeply. No matter how good the replacement was, the gap felt huge.

Our grief and immaturity clashed with their experience and logic.

People hurting felt annoyed by those "trying to lead".

Neither side was wrong—they were just in different places in the story.

But it didn't feel like their side was the best at communicating.

Here's what I want you to consider: When a group loses a ministry leader to death, it's not just a position to be filled.

It's a life to be honored.

And *"quick honor"* rarely feels like authentic honor.

I also noticed something else in my peers—a curious shift that I could only call clarity or denial.

When a leader dies, there's a natural urge to walk forward confidently. Maybe we think it's God's way of telling us, *"You're ready for the next step."*

There are questions without answers—things we won't fully understand this side of heaven.

And that's okay.

But so much mystery and disappointment makes some people **act confident too fast.**

That confidence can leave others still grieving feeling overlooked and bulldozed.

This isn't moving on. It's skipping over.

And no one who loves a leader wants that.

Ministry leaders who pass on leave more than assignments. They leave principles.

Even if some were easier to see than others.

So if someone dies and leaves you without clear next steps, the best move is **patient conversation.**

Make your decisions. Turn the page.

But do it under the umbrella of understanding and perspective.

Decisions don't wait for perfect deciders—even if we wish they did. But beyond *"perfect,"* there's a right way to move forward.

And we should take the time to find it.

———————————————————

The second category of **failure** is one we touched on in the first chapter. But this time, it's from the vantage point of dealing with the loss of someone on your team or ministry **because of their failure.**

Beyond the failure itself — beyond the unveiling and the damage that ripples through your community and their trust.

I've seen ministers of many ages say they've felt betrayed — sometimes by people they were close to, **sometimes by people they never even met** — because of those failures.

Affairs, embezzlement, manipulation... the list goes on.

For many, this is just a sad reality.
For others, it sparks anger.

How could someone with so much potential and favor throw it all away for momentary satisfaction?

And the hardest part?

It's not just the failure itself... it's the aftermath.

That gnawing question: *"Was everything they ever did in ministry... or taught us... just hollow? Meaningless?"*

Has this ever happened to you?

Where a leader poured wisdom into your life, only for you to watch their life fall apart because **they didn't follow their own advice?**

It's natural to want to throw out the advice with the advice-giver.

If it came from them, **could it really have been genuine truth?**

This reminds me of Saul and David — one of the most dysfunctional mentor-mentee relationships in the Bible.

On one page, Saul is God's chosen king and leader of the people.

A few pages later, David steps into that role — Saul's disobedience and insecurity having created chaos that David now must clean up.

Saul's public failure left a stain on his life forever.

People probably said things like, ***"How embarrassing for him,"*** or, ***"I bet God regrets ever using him."***

But David?

He's repeatedly put in situations where he could take revenge, but chooses another path.

He passes the test.

Scripture tells us Saul tried to kill David out of jealousy.

One time, Saul took a bathroom break in a cave — and David was hiding there. David saw his chance to change the story Saul had written in his mind about him. So, he sneaks up and cuts off a corner of Saul's robe — just to prove he could harm him if he wanted to.

But David doesn't.

1 Samuel 24:5-8 says: *"Afterward, David was conscience-stricken for having cut off a corner of his robe. He said to his men, 'The Lord forbid that I should do such a thing to my master, the Lord's anointed, or lay my hand on him; for he is the anointed of the Lord.'"*

How wild is that?

David felt horrible — not because he'd hurt Saul, but because he even allowed himself to think about it.

It wasn't about the act — even cutting the robe was crossing a line for him.

But here's the kicker: The people around David were convinced this was God's green light for David to kill Saul.

They saw it as divine justice.
It had to be!

That narrative — that someone's failure means we can write off their entire past and future — is one I've heard over and over again.

Suddenly, someone we called brother or sister becomes the subject of jokes in staff meetings, gossip in conversations, and disbelief in our hearts.

We know what they did.

And we treat it like a license to pretend God never called them in the first place.

Having someone leave badly creates a mess.
A mess we have to clean up.

It can lead to conversations that don't just question your abilities, **but also your team, your ministry, even your faith.**

That mess makes you want to vent.
And venting can easily slip into slander.

Our anger comes from disappointment.

And disappointment? It's rooted in hurt.

But I urge you — take the David road.

Never let someone's failure cloud your eyes to the God who first called them.

Even if they aren't serving God now, **they once did.**

They once cried real tears.
They once felt a real calling.

They made mistakes, yes. Maybe they won't reach the same influence again. **But that doesn't mean their story is over.**

WHAT'S BEST IS NEXT

Sometimes the best thing that can happen is for someone to move on and start fresh — for them, and for the ministry they are leaving.

It's never easy, but time does what it's famous for: healing wounds.

Healing isn't automatic. **It takes intention.**

Even if you never minister together again, you can still believe in a healthy future for everyone.

The third category of **growth** is one I think doesn't get talked about enough — but it might be the simplest to grasp.

Did you know a plant in a pot will grow only so much... **and then**

stop?

Years go by. No growth. No change.

There's only one way to restart that growth: move it to a bigger pot.

Once that happens, growth reignites — **until it reaches the limits of the new pot.**

This cycle repeats until the plant has no more pots to move to.

Sometimes when people leave, **it's not because anything bad happened.**

**No one failed. No one died.
It's just time to change pots.**

A plant doesn't blame its pot for holding it back. It simply sees its limits and understands what needs to happen next.

We need to be the same.

Whether we're the ones leaving or the ones watching others go.

I've noticed ministers often think, *"I have to hold onto what I have because I might never get more."*

Volunteers aren't always abundant.
Talent isn't always available.
Budgets aren't always bountiful.

So it's natural to want to hold tight to the people you know, trust, and love.

But when someone finds the courage to step into the unknown, **they should feel our championing voice behind them.**

They're probably more scared than we are.

And the truth is — God is a God of abundance.

I've seen countless stories of people leaving, only for *"more amazing"* people to show up right after.

People leave. We leave.

It's natural.

We rarely get to control the how or when — but we can control **how we respond** when we find ourselves next to their empty seat.

That seat isn't empty because it's meant to stay that way.

It's empty because someone perfect for it is **on their way.**

So when people leave—**whatever the reason**—let's respond with patience in our communication, honor as we clean up what's left behind, and openness to whatever God has next.

At the end of the day, fighting the memories of those who aren't here anymore?

That's a dangerous routine for our wellbeing.

Plus, it just looks plain crazy :)

CHAPTER ELEVEN

REMEMBER WHAT YOU CAN'T

staying the course

You've made it all the way to the end of this book, **and I couldn't be more impressed!**

I know some of my analogies can seem bizarre, my stories feel unique, and my principles might be difficult to swallow at best.

But what I said at the beginning — **I want you to survive working for God** — that truly rings in my heart behind every word I've written.

I want you to approach ministry with confidence and conviction, but also with realistic expectations of what could happen beyond theology and Sunday services.

I want the puzzles of personalities, the navigation of drama, and the perspective of opinions all to culminate in you **keeping your joy in serving.**

You tend to have to balance all these things in your mind at the same time, which can be difficult.

Hence the title of this chapter: *"Remember What You Can't."*

I'm sure, like a lot of other things I've said throughout this book, you may think that statement doesn't make sense.

How do we remember something we can't remember?

What I mean is there are things we don't remember because we simply don't, and then there are things we can't remember **because we're too overwhelmed to even consider them.**

For example, if we stress about finances more and more, our trust in God's faithful provision — both in scripture and in our lives — will feel less and less anchored.

I remember when I first wanted to start waking up early in the morning.

It's about as opposite to my personality as you can go.

That, by the way, had a lot to do with why it took me so long to graduate from college. But I'd reached a point where I wanted to make some adjustments — to prioritize the new season I was in.

I'd only been married a short time, but I quickly realized I no longer lived in a world where I could just hide in a back room and work until three in the morning.

And honestly?
That was a good thing.

But where would I get that time back?

I needed more hours in the day, and the only place I could find them was in the morning. So, I put on my big boy pants and set an alarm.

Now, I don't want to brag, but **I am an award-winning snooze button champion.**

I don't want to say undefeated — that's stretching it — but not by much.

I wanted to change that, **but it took several attempts.**

First, I set the alarm at max volume.
No luck.

Then I put it in a far-away room where I'd have to get out of bed to turn it off.

The only progress?

Learning to deal with cold feet while crawling back into bed.

Then I tried two alarms — one by the bed and one in the kitchen a few minutes later — so the whole house would remind me of my commitment to early rising.

Still didn't work.
And I began to realize why.

My determination to wake up early only mattered to me the day before — when I saw how many things were falling through the cracks.

But in the morning?
I couldn't remember that frustration.

I only remembered the feeling of my nice, warm bed.

What I remembered the most won the moment.

So I went to Walmart and bought some poster board. I made signs to surround my phone that said things like, *"Stay up, stupid!"* *(This is true.)*

There were whiteboards and post-it notes, too.
One even said, *"Remember what you can't."*

I knew the real issue, and that made it easier to **place a target on what I had to conquer.**

To this day, the alarm on my phone still says it.
(Just not the "stupid" part.)

When people survive in ministry for a long time, it's usually for one of two reasons: They got intentional — or they got calloused.

I don't want us to become the latter.

Too many ministers have become bitter and/or numb. That's not what God intended when He called us into ministry, whether we serve every day or only once in a while.

You may end up working for God a long time, but that's not the ultimate goal.

If it was, it would be a *"by any means necessary"* situation.

What we're looking for is longevity hand-in-hand with love for God and love for people — **not toleration.**

I've seen people do ministry **in spite of people.**

And while that might make sense on paper, I also think God looks at it as foolishness. God sees the world and the people in it and thinks: **That is worth giving up my Son for.**

The most precious thing to Him was sacrificed so those people could know Him.

That doesn't sound like a tolerating attitude.

But it also doesn't sound like someone naive to the challenges those people will present either. The people Jesus came to save are the exact same people who mocked His sacrifice to His face.

If anyone has the right to retire from the work of ministry, I'd say Jesus has the strongest argument.

But this is when Jesus asks His Father to forgive people — **for being people.**

With all of our amazing qualities and gifts, we can also be moody, unrealistic, flighty, clicky, deceptive, greedy — and that's all before you get into the real nitty gritty.

Jesus sees it all at once and still chooses forgiveness—not because it's earned, but because He remembers what His Father saw when He sent Him.

He holds on to what we can so easily forget.

1 Corinthians 13:7 says, *"Love always protects, always trusts, always hopes, always perseveres."*

Love isn't just flowers and rainbows.
Love has grit.

Love can look trials in the face and still persevere — all because it knows there's an end worth getting to.

Maybe when you observe ministers, you don't always see someone who persevered.

And that scares you.

Maybe you saw someone who appeared to love money more than people. Or you sat in meetings where **love was the last thing invited to the table.**

Your memory is scarred by it.

Or you had a loved one who was chewed up and spit out by a *"mega ministry machine,"* and their wounds now feel like your own.

These aren't feelings that need to be swept under the rug or pushed aside *"for the sake of the Gospel."*

They need to be addressed — both personally and corporately — for the sake of the Gospel.

That might not happen as soon as we think it needs to, or as efficiently as we'd like, but we can all start somewhere.

Reading this book, hopefully, is a step in that direction.

It's silly to assume this book is the one-stop cure for ministry wounds and premature retirement.

The Word of God has more healing and wisdom in a single sentence than I could muster in a thousand books.

And frankly, that should relieve us all.

CAREER BENEFITS

I'm an observer by nature, so I know what it's like to spend your life seeing things that are never explained—leaving you to try to figure out their actions and meanings.

This leaves you guessing, not discovering the truth.

Even if sometimes, things happen to line up just right.

At one point or another, we ALL have a reason why we should quit working for God.

Even if we haven't started yet, we've seen enough proof in others that it might not be the right *"career path"* for us.

But I want you to imagine all the people who might be impacted by your ministry.

Whatever that ministry is, however you do it, wherever you are.

For me, I've written worship songs, and it's been one of the craziest experiences to see people impacted by them.

I've lost count of the times I've watched someone sing a song with very little outward emotion... only for another song to open the floodgates of tears and gratitude.

The outward expression isn't the point, because I've also met people who don't show any emotion, but inside, their hearts are exploding with love toward God.

That's an important reminder.

But when I see someone moved by a song, **I can't help but think about what that moment means to God.**

Who knows that person's story? What they've been through, what they've overcome, what it even took just to be in that room, singing that song?

In this small moment, we get a glimpse into their surrender and love for God—**who's been their anchor and sustainer through it all.**

Someone wrote the words that helped create that moment.

Anyone could've written the song.
Any song could've been sung.

But it was that specific one.

For some reason, God is right there in the middle of that moment in a special way.

Now imagine if the writer of that song could watch that happen.

I bet they'd have a brand new appreciation for all the work it took to write it... and all it took to get through the mountains and valleys of their own life just to write it in the first place.

It would be special.
It would be sacred.
It would be worth it.

That's how I want us to think about ministry.

The hard truth?

We won't always get to see the actual fruit of our labor in this way.

Sometimes, we catch glimpses, but never the full picture we want.

But guess who does?
God.

God gets a front-row seat to all the amazing fruit that comes from our trees.

Paul said it best in 1 Corinthians 3:6: *"I planted, Apollos watered, but God gave the increase."*

Paul did what he could with his time—using what he learned from fellow believers and even parts of his story before he was saved.

Then others came and did the same.

They brought their gifts, stories, and life experiences to add to the work.

But at the end of the day, only one person made any of it fruitful.

That was God.

God sees our story beyond the surface. **He holds our hand at the beginning... and cheers us on at the finish line.**

We can share that same heart for one another.

"Therefore encourage one another and build each other up, just as in fact you are doing." (1 Thessalonians 5:11)

If I could leave you with one piece of advice on how to survive working for God, it would be this: **believe you can.**

And then encourage those who no longer believe they can.

This journey is long—**and often lonely.**

But we can be living proof that it's worth it.

We can be the *"Billy Graham"* visiting someone in their pit of despair. The one who passes their test, sets a new example, helps others grow, treats people with respect—and more.

Before long, new memories form.

Memories of hundreds joining the ministry every week—**not leaving it.**

Incredible ministers being commended for their integrity instead of paraded for their faults.

I know that's a hard reality to imagine...
And if I'm honest, that's exactly why I enjoy imagining it.

Ministry is worth every ounce of effort you put into it.

When Jesus is the rock you're built on, the waves of everything else simply can't compete.

So, on behalf of your future self, **thank you for reading this book.**

Thank you for the people who will see the Kingdom of God just a little clearer because of your life and sacrifices.

God gave us His Son—not for nothing, but for a purpose.

A reward of people choosing the Author of Love over everything else.

Your *"yes"* to serving His people and His house is part of that reward.

And your Father is glad you said it.

Here's to surviving the best job in the world!

PRAYER

A closing moment for our time together.

Jesus, I thank You that You're involved in this reader's story.

I thank You that You don't just call us to work for You—you call us into a co-laboring relationship, one whose burden is easy and light.

I bless this reader's mind—their family, their finances, their friendships. I bless both the fruitful places bursting at the seams and the broken areas that have barely seen new seeds begin to grow.

I thank You that You love them beyond how well or poorly they perform.

I bless their imagination: that they would become distracted by the daydreams of Heaven, and that they would see the goodness of the Lord in the land where they are currently living.

I thank You that they are precious in Your sight.

I pray Your joy would strengthen them to endure, Your peace would hold them in confusion, and Your kindness would keep them in repentance.

Let them love You more on their last breath than on any other day before it.

Thank You for who they are and what You've made them to be.

Amen.

WORDS I NEED TO SAY

Some things can't be processed in bullet points or checklists. Sometimes, they need to be written in the form of a letter.

This is your space to do that.

Choose one (**or all**) of the options below, and write as honestly as you can. Don't worry about grammar or getting it *"right."* This isn't for anyone else's eyes—it's for you and God.

Let it be raw. Let it be real. Let it be healing.

You can write:
• **A letter to your younger self** — the version of you who didn't see this coming.
• **A letter to someone who hurt you** — the person who disappointed, betrayed, or left.
• **A letter to God** — honest, unfiltered, and from right where you are.

These letters aren't for sending. They're for releasing.

Keep them, tear them up, or burn them **if you're feeling epic**—whatever helps you let go.

It's okay to pause, cry, or come back later.
This isn't about finishing.

It's about naming what's been buried—**and letting God meet you there.**

JOURNAL PROMPTS

Take your time. These prompts aren't a checklist—
they're a space to process honestly with God.

You can go through them one by one or sit with the ones that
speak the loudest. There's no rush and no right answers.

Let them lead you into deeper reflection, healing, and clarity.

Be real. Be present. Let God meet you there.

1. When was the last time you felt unseen or unrecognized—but knew you were still called? What did that feel like?

2. Are there any areas where you've been reacting out of pain instead of responding in partnership with God?

3. Where have you built walls instead of boundaries? What's one wall God might be inviting you to lower?

4. What promise are you holding right now that feels heavy or delayed? How is God shaping your character in the waiting?

5. Is there a person or situation where God is asking you to let them fail—not out of neglect, but so growth can actually happen?

6. Who are the "ghosts" you're still trying to fight? What would it take to release them?

7. What's one thing you need to forgive yourself for in leadership?

8. What's something you want to remember about God's faithfulness in this season—even if you can't fully see it yet?

9. After reading this book, do you feel more equipped to survive working for God? If yes/no, how so?

10. Picture yourself decades from now—still walking with God, still faithful, fulfilled, and at peace. What would that future version of you say to encourage you in this current season?

SURVIVAL MAP

A checklist to stay faithful, healthy, and grounded in who God called you to be.

1. Identity — *Who are you—really?*
Do you know who you are in God, and are you living and leading from that place?

✓ Are you anchored in identity, not approval?
✓ Are you acting according to conviction, not pressure?

2. Serving — *Can you serve where you're not seen?*
Do you feel free to serve a vision that isn't fully your own—and do it with joy?

✓ Can you follow as faithfully as you lead?
✓ Can you honor what you don't control?

3. Health — *Are you tending to your heart?*
Are you paying attention to your emotions, limits, and inner world—not just the outcomes?

✓ Are you living with healthy boundaries, not hidden burnout?
✓ Are you leading from a place of overflow, not depletion?

4. Longevity — *Do you have a plan to last?*
Survival isn't accidental. Do you have rhythms, people, and practices that help you stay faithful over time?

✓ Are you building sustainability, not just momentum?
✓ Do you have long-term vision, not just short-term fire?

YOU WERE NEVER MEANT TO CARRY MINISTRY ALONE.

PASTORS, WORSHIP LEADERS, CREATIVES, VOLUNTEERS, PRODUCTION TEAMS, COMMUNICATORS, AND CHURCH STAFFS EVERYWHERE ARE CARRYING MORE THAN MOST PEOPLE REALIZE.

THAT'S WHY **THE WORKING FOR GOD COLLECTIVE** EXISTS.

WFG© IS AN ONGOING MEMBERSHIP AND COMMUNITY BUILT FOR CHURCHES AND MINISTRY TEAMS WHO WANT TO STAY HEALTHY, UNIFIED, AND SERVING GOD WITHOUT BURNING OUT.

INSIDE, YOU'LL FIND:

- MONTHLY TEACHINGS AND FRESH TRAINING MATERIALS
- COURSES AND PRACTICAL MINISTRY TOOLS
- LEADERSHIP AND TEAM HEALTH RESOURCES
- HONEST CONVERSATIONS WITH PEOPLE WHO UNDERSTAND
- A GROWING NETWORK OF CHURCHES AND LEADERS AROUND THE WORLD WALKING THROUGH THE SAME THINGS YOU ARE

WHETHER YOU SERVE ON STAGE, BEHIND THE SCENES, OR ANYWHERE IN BETWEEN—**YOU BELONG HERE.**

SCAN THE QR CODE TO GET STARTED!

JOIN WFG!!!!

LOOKING FOR MORE RESOURCES?

We offer digital courses, consulting, team development, mentoring, and additional services designed to help churches and ministry teams stay healthy and grow stronger together!

VISIT US AT
WORKINGFORGOD.CO

(that's ".co" <u>NOT</u> ".com")

+ FOLLOW US ON SOCIALS
@WEWORKINGFORGOD

We can't wait to run with you!

ABOUT THE AUTHOR

Tyler Richardson is a writer, dreamer, and most of all, a proud dad to his daughter, Banner Woods, and husband to Kennedy Gabrielle, who keep his heart full and life inspired.

He also enjoys cinnamon altoids, music, fasion, culture, daydreaming, old Disney Channel Original Movies, and overpriced lattes.

He'd also like to personally thank you for buying this book... so more lattes may be purchased for himself and Kennedy. :)

Steeples, crowds, and fame will fade—but Jesus. There's the way.